ONE-DESIGN
RACING

TECHNIQUES OF ONE-DESIGN RACING

JACK EVANS

Edited and Illustrated by
RANDALL DE LEEUW

Haessner
PUBLISHING, INC.

Library of Congress Catalog Card No.: 75-18555
ISBN 0-87799-043-3

All text and captions are set in Helios.
Book edited, illustrated and
designed by **Randall De Leeuw**

Haessner Publishing, Inc.
Newfoundland, New Jersey 07435

Printed in the United States of America

CONTENTS

Editor's Note

I met Jack Evans twice before we began work on this book -- first when he lectured at the Green Pond Yacht Club and then again on the race course at Crystal Lake, Connecticut. The combination of his style as lecturer (he talked, I listened) and racer (he finished first, I finished third) convinced me that a book by Jack had to be a winner. Hence the collaboration --**Techniques of One-Design Racing**.

I have attempted to keep both the text and illustrations as clear, simple and direct as possible. Words in bold face type can be found in the glossary. The illustrations are located as close to the text reference as possible.

I want to thank Walt Haessner for his interest in, patience with and encouragement of this book. Please advise us of any additions or corrections which you may come across in reading this volume. We welcome your interest.

Randall De Leeuw
Green Pond, N.J. July, 1975

Preface

Sailing is a sport of integrity, good competition and lasting friendships. Sailors freely exchange ideas and thoughts and are always willing to assist a fellow sailor. Without this kind of special relationship, **Techniques of One-Design Racing** would not have been possible. I would like to thank my fellow sailors and in particular Randall De Leeuw for his boundless talents and patience, AMF Alcort for the use of the Sunfish and Force 5 in our photographs, Phillip Saccio for his professional photographic skills, Will White for his analysis of the working proofs of this text and Walt Haessner for encouragement and undying enthusiasm. Finally, I must thank my wife and family for their steadfast support, interest and enthusiasm during this project.

I hope when reading this book you enjoy it as much as I enjoyed writing it. I had fun with this project and learned even more about the sport of sailing. Maybe this is why the sport of sailing is a never ceasing challenge. One can never learn everything.

Jack Evans
Waterbury, Ct. July, 1975

1 INTRODUCTION

In early sailboat racing all one had to do to win was build a yacht which was faster than everyone else's. This generally meant the biggest yacht because it was well known that a big yacht was faster than a small yacht. This led to a building war - each owner wanted the biggest and fastest yacht. In a nutshell this was the start of the "Sport of Kings" - only the very wealthy could afford to build a new yacht every year and incur the expense of design, construction, crew and upkeep.

Fortunately, early in the sport many sailors realized the need for handicaping large yachts to allow the smaller boats to be competitive. With this came racing rules and eventually the development of one-design sailboat racing. This later occurance opened sailboat racing to a large number of "Kings." One-design sailboat racing means that everyone is racing in a yacht which is of the same design. This reduces the cost of owning and racing a boat because the developmental and design costs are almost eliminated and the boats can be mass produced. In recent years there has been a further refinement of the one-design concept to that of the single manufacturer one-design. This means that only one builder produces a given design.

Most one-design racing is done in small, light weight craft. This is the type of boat you are most likely involved with and, to me, provides the most interesting type of sailboat racing. You are continually required to develop the most out of your boat and yourself.

Early in my racing career I made a startling discovery - all boats in a one-design class are not the same. The term one-design was somewhat misleading. I had discovered that from boat to boat there were a number of subtle differences. This bothered me. I felt in a true one-design class everyone should have the same advantages, and the differences I discovered meant that some people were sailing a faster boat than mine. It was easier to rationalize losing to a sailor with a new boat and expensive equipment, for obviously with those advantages he should be winning.

But this cloud of contentment was thoroughly shattered when I attended a regatta and the winning boat was twice as old as mine. The winner had holes in its sails and virtually sank between races. Losing to a boat in that condition was a bitter pill. Then it dawned on me that it wasn't a faster boat I was losing to but rather a faster sailer. It was easy for me to admit that someone with a new boat, sails and expensive gear could beat me. But admit a better sailor could? That's tough. Obviously, then, the key in one-design racing is to be the fastest sailor.

The hardest thing about sailboat racing is trying to explain what makes one boat of a given design faster than another boat of the same design. Whenever the question is asked, sailors will spend hours, days and even years presenting theories, reasons and justifications in explanation. Much of the time they forget the single biggest factor on the boat - *the sailor*. If the sailor is fast, he will more than make up for minor differences between boats.

This book has been put together to help show you what you can do to make yourself a faster sailor. If you become faster it follows that your boat will become faster too! I will not try to present long justifications of why certain techniques work. Rather, I will present a number of ideas and tendencies which you should try. Remember, everyone sails differently and therefore there are no absolute adjustments or techniques that everyone should use. This book is divided into two sections. The first is a discussion of beating, reaching and running. In this section I present a number of ideas and techniques which allow you to tune both the boat and yourself for maximum efficiency and power, in other words, the techniques of a fast sailor. The second section aims this fast sailor on a model race course.

As we begin this first section remember, there are no absolutes in sailing. A technique one sailor swears by another may swear at. It is important to develop techniques that are efficient for you and constantly maintain the theory that it is the sailor that makes the boat fast. In this way you will start making the same decisions and adjustments the winners are making and, in turn, your boat will be as fast as theirs.

2 BEATING

There are three main components used to make sail adjustments while beating -- the **cunningham**, **outhaul** and **mainsheet**. Most people tend to pull the cunningham and outhaul tight for upwind sailing and then rely solely on the mainsheet to let the sail in and out as they become over-powered during gusts. However, adjustments to the sail made with the cunningham and outhaul can be of equal importance to those of the mainsheet, critically effecting sail shape and performance. In general, one wants his sail and rig to produce slightly more power than can be comfort-ably handled for the given conditions. If you adjusted your sail so that it was producing slightly less power than you can handle comfortably, you would be essentially driving a car which was slightly underpowered. So how do we go about adjusting the sail to create such power? First, we look for a sail that creates a balance between outhaul, cunningham and mainsheet tension.

For the given conditions, first adjust the cunningham to the point where you begin to remove the wrinkles along the mast. Then simply ease the outhaul until you become slightly overpowered. This sounds quite simple. However, there are some other adjustments to take in consider-ation. First, overtightening the cunningham will pull to sail draft forward and create a large deep curve directly behind the mast (Figure 1 & 2). This large curve prevents one from pointing. As the wind passes over the mast it will strike this deep curve behind the mast causing the sail to luff (Figure 3 & 4). To eliminate the luff, one must bear away slightly to fill the sail (Figure 5).

Easing the outhaul simply adds draft to the sail -- and drafts means power. Simply put, the **cunningham** controls the luff tension of the sail and the location of the draft fore and aft. The **outhaul** controls the amount of

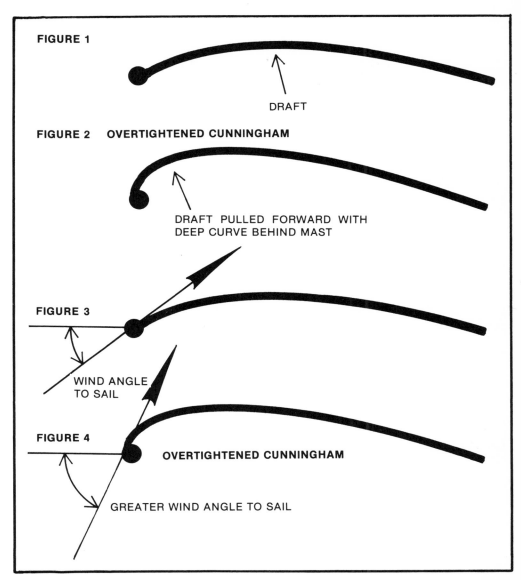

FIGURE 1

DRAFT

FIGURE 2   OVERTIGHTENED CUNNINGHAM

DRAFT PULLED FORWARD WITH
DEEP CURVE BEHIND MAST

FIGURE 3

WIND ANGLE
TO SAIL

FIGURE 4

OVERTIGHTENED CUNNINGHAM

GREATER WIND ANGLE TO SAIL

draft or the amount of power the sail can produce. Now add mainsheet
tension. The mast will begin to bend and your sail adjustments will need
modifying to account for this added force.

It is helpful to know how a sail is constructed. In general, a sail is
given draft by the sail maker. He does this in a combination of two ways.
He can tailor each individual sail panel (make each seam curved instead of
straight) and he can add draft to the sail by increasing or decreasing the **luff
curve** and/or the **foot curve** (Figure 6 & 7). When these curved edges are put

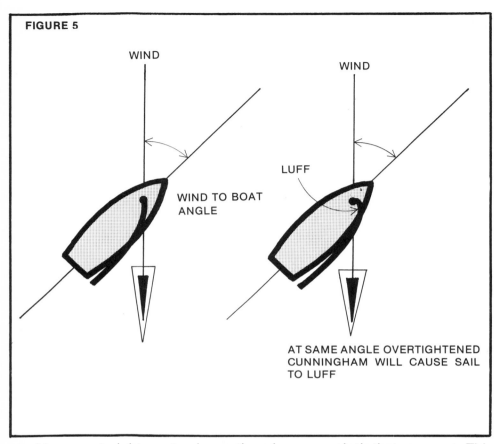

FIGURE 5

WIND

WIND

LUFF

WIND TO BOAT
ANGLE

AT SAME ANGLE OVERTIGHTENED
CUNNINGHAM WILL CAUSE SAIL
TO LUFF

next to your straight mast or boom there is excess cloth that sags out. This excess is a sail's draft. This is a very simple explanation of a very complex art, but essentially the sail maker is trying to produce a powerful sail which will point very high and will be flexible for all wind conditions. With a properly developed sail, the use of cunninghams and outhauls, mast bends and mainsheet tensions allows a skipper a great deal of flexibility for a wide range of wind conditions.

By adjusting the cunningham, outhaul and mainsheet we are attempting to achieve a symmetry which will produce efficient power. As you tighten the mainsheet, the mast will begin to bend and approximate the shape of the luff curve of the sail (Figure 8). As this happens not only does the overall draft of the sail begin to diminish, but the leading edge of the sail is drawn flat and the boat will begin to point closer to the wind (Figure 9).

When beating, set the sail to produce as much power as can be used efficiently. Generally this will mean being slightly over-powered. The "fast sailor" is constantly trying to adjust his sail and rig to produce as much

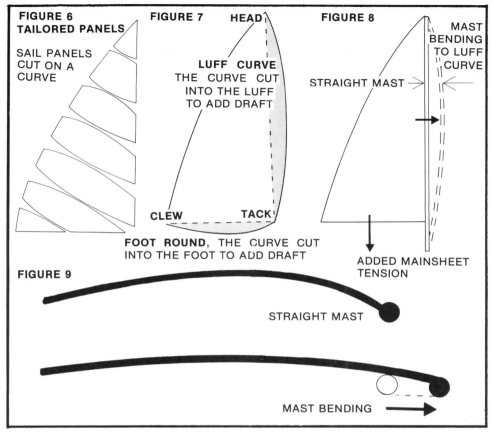

FIGURE 6
TAILORED PANELS

SAIL PANELS CUT ON A CURVE

FIGURE 7 HEAD

LUFF CURVE
THE CURVE CUT INTO THE LUFF TO ADD DRAFT

CLEW TACK

FOOT ROUND, THE CURVE CUT INTO THE FOOT TO ADD DRAFT

FIGURE 8

MAST BENDING TO LUFF CURVE

STRAIGHT MAST

ADDED MAINSHEET TENSION

FIGURE 9

STRAIGHT MAST

MAST BENDING

power as can possibly be used. This is why you will see him continually adjusting his sail to find the maximum point of power.

Next we come to the use of the **traveler**. When one becomes overpowered on a boat which does not have a traveler, the skipper simply eases the mainsheet, which in turn spills air from the sail. However, easing the mainsheet destroys the symmetry that was established with the cunningham, outhaul and mainsheet adjustments. When the gust is over or when you are able to pull in the mainsheet you must spend an extra moment to assure yourself that your mainsheet adjustment is close to the adjustment you had before the gust. You must be careful not to **oversheet** (pull in the mainsheet too far) and thereby distort the spars to the point where the sail will no longer propel the boat forward and result in an oversheeted and stalled condition.

Oversheeting turns the boat into a large windvane. As the sail approaches the centerline of the boat, the boat begins to pivot about the board and point into the wind. When this happens the skipper's first inclination is to steer away from the wind, pulling hard on the tiller. The

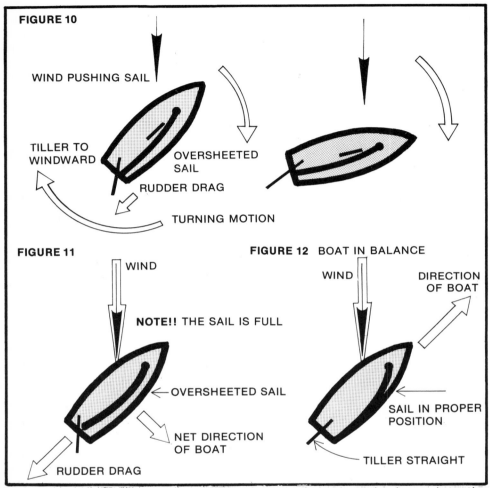

FIGURE 10

WIND PUSHING SAIL

TILLER TO
WINDWARD

OVERSHEETED
SAIL

RUDDER DRAG

TURNING MOTION

FIGURE 11

WIND

NOTE!! THE SAIL IS FULL

OVERSHEETED SAIL

NET DIRECTION
OF BOAT

RUDDER DRAG

FIGURE 12 BOAT IN BALANCE

WIND

DIRECTION
OF BOAT

SAIL IN PROPER
POSITION

TILLER STRAIGHT

moment this motion is induced the aft end of the boat is drawn into the wind, and as it comes into the wind the sail trys to push it away from the wind and the boat stops (Figure 10). When you are in this configuration the boat literally slides sideways as it has no forward motion. The sail is a large flat plane pushing the boat sideways and the rudder is acting as a huge brake (Figure 11). The first rule to remember if your boat stops sailing is **ease the mainsheet**. Easing the mainsheet will put everything back into balance and the boat will begin to sail forward (Figure 12). The second thing that comes in handy is to **steer away from the wind**. When caught in a stalled condition, the boat is pointed very close to the wind. By easing the mainsheet and steering away from the wind the boat will begin to accelerate and once again sail properly.

In a boat with a mid-boom sheeting system and a full width traveler, easing the sheet is an entirely different matter. To spill air (and thereby decrease power), ease the traveler rather than the mainsheet. By using the traveler instead of the mainsheet, one does not disturb the relationship between the cunningham, outhaul and mainsheet. Rather, the sail opens and closes like a huge door before the wind. By easing the traveler, the sail door opens and spills wind. Retrieving the traveler will close the door, increase power, and propel the boat forward. This is a very positive and almost instantaneous control for on and off power. The advantage in using the traveler: one only has to move a foot or two of traveler control line. To get the same boom movement with the mainsheet could take as much as twelve feet of line. It is much quicker to retrieve two feet of line than twelve.

How do you set the traveler? In the middle, to one side, slightly to one side? Just how? The traveler is generally a indication of where the boom lies in relation to the boat. On most boats the traveler is set amidships or slightly to leeward while beating. On occasion the traveler may be to windward because when you set your sail for lighter air you may not want to bend the mast. In this case mainsheet tension will be quite light. By drawing the traveler to windward you pull the sail into its proper position for beating. As the wind increases, you add mainsheet tension. The boom will then begin to align itself over the traveler as the mast begins to bend. If the traveler remained to windward the boom would either approach or cross the centerline of the boat. The sail would be oversheeted and induce a stalled condition. To correct this, ease the traveler to amidships or slightly to leeward. The boom will move to its normal position in relationship to the boat (Figure 13).

It is important to note that I have not given specific adjustments, such as adjust the cunningham two inches here, the outhaul two inches there, or the mainsheet be set with blocks sixteen inches apart. Everyone sails a boat differently. What is correct for me is not necessarily correct for you, your neighbor, or someone else. **You** have to adjust **your** boat to produce the power that **you** can use. By showing you the adjustments which other sailors are making and how and why they are going about it, you can learn to adjust your boat for your own style of sailing.

Hull trim is the next important area to be discussed. Most sailors feel that by making a few adjustments to the sail and a few good wind shift selections upwind, everything will be alright. However, hull trim is a very subtle area of boat speed, and in dinghy racing plays an important part in adjusting the helm of the boat. Put very simply, the further forward you move the more you tend to induce **weather helm** (that is, induce the boat to steer itself into the wind). The further aft you move the more you tend to induce **lee helm** (that is, allow the boat to steer away from the wind). Let's look at this in greater depth.

It is extremely useful to study your hull from the bottom side. By

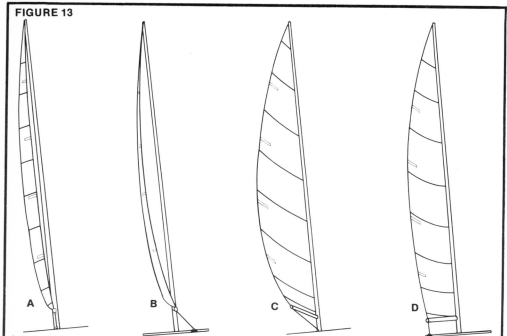

FIGURE 13

A In light air with the traveler set amidships, the sail aligns itself over the boom causing the sail leech to "hook" to windward and capture wind in the sail.

B By adjusting the traveler to windward, you can ease the mainsheet just enough to allow the boom to raise slightly. This boom rise permits the sail leech tension to relax and in turn permit the wind to flow across the sail.

C In heavy air with the traveler amidships, you must ease the mainsheet to compensate for the wind. This in turn allows the leech to twist excessively, thus destroying the efficient, powerful shape of the sail.

D By easing the traveler to compensate for the higher wind velocity, you can tighten the mainsheet and in turn the sail leech, thus returning the sail to its efficient, powerful shape. In medium air one must adjust the sail and traveler between these two extremes and establish a symmetry between all the sail adjustments.

inverting the boat on your lawn, you will gain a good perspective of what type of hull you are trying to push through the water. If possible, get to an elevated vantage point. Try to determine whether your hull is full forward or full aft, whether the bow will be deep to the water or just below the surface. These are relative terms, but by observing the hull from different vantage points you will soon learn some basic things.

For example, a **Sunfish** can be classified as a "cods head mackerel tail" type hull configuration - the bow is very full while the transom and after areas are very narrow. Compare this to a **Laser**, which is somewhat thinner forward and tends to carry its fullness further aft. Finally, compare these two with a **Force 5**, which is even narrower forward and carries its fullness even further aft. A broad flat area will float more easily, as it will support a given load more readily than a sharp, narrow one.

After you have determined where the fullness of your boat is located, launch the boat and see how it floats. Put a crew on board and have them move under your direction. A hull which is full forward generally requires the crew weight well forward. This allows the fullness of the hull to carry the load. But if the weight is placed too far aft, the fullness will not support any load, and the bow will be easily moved by wind and waves and the boat will slide sideways. Moving your crew while at the dock will tell you if your predictions are correct. A hull which is narrow forward will keep its bow down when weight is moved forward, be less effected by wave motion, and will tend to slice through the waves rather than be knocked aside by them.

Noting the undershape of your hull will help determine the best place to locate your weight. While beating, place your weight slightly forward of the maximum fullness area. This will keep the bow down and prevent it from being knocked around by the wind and waves.

In extremely light air it is most helpful to keep your weight well forward, inducing the leeward bow wave and transom sideslide effect. As you move forward, your weight depresses the bow and lifts the stern, allowing the transom of the boat to slide sideways. A deeply depressed bow will induce a large leeward bow wave pushing the bow into the wind. This provides two things essential for light air performance -- induced weather helm and an anti-side-slip (leeway) effect. As the leeward bow wave is trying to push the bow into the wind, you must have the rudder offset to prevent this motion, and hence this rudder trys to lift the transom into the wind. Essentially you are lifting both ends of the boat into the wind. If you stay in this same forward position as the wind increases, the weather helm will become so overpowering that instead of lifting the boat to windward the offset rudder will act as a break, stop the boat, and cause you to heel more. Thus it is necessary to move aft along the hull as the wind increases, thereby reducing the helm and keeping the boat on its feet.

For most dinghy racing it is a good idea to keep the boat flat, side to side. Most sailors feel that a slight heel is better than sailing flat as this reduces the amount of hull surface in the water, reducing the frictional drag of the water rolling along the hull. However, excess heeling is extremely costly in high performance sailing. Once the boat begins to heel too far one begins to lift the board and rudder out of the water and reduce the **lateral resistance plane** (the area projected by the board, rudder and hull which prevents the boat from sailing sideways). With the boat well heeled the leeway is increased and one feels a stronger weather helm. To counteract this, one pulls harder on the tiller. On an angle and offset, the rudder tends to lift the transom out of the water and further increase the weather helm to a point which can stop the boat's motion. One adjusts this side to side hull trim by what is known as **hiking**.

TIGHTEN THE LUFF (CUNNINGHAM) TO REMOVE WRINKLES.

WRINKLE REMOVED ALONG THE LUFF.

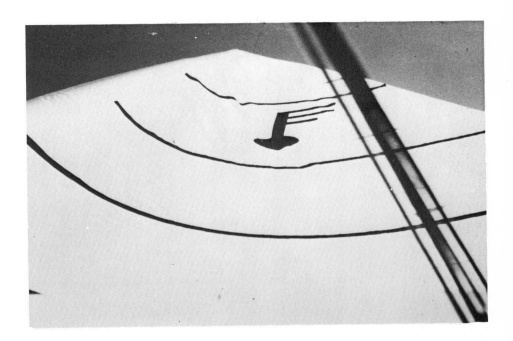

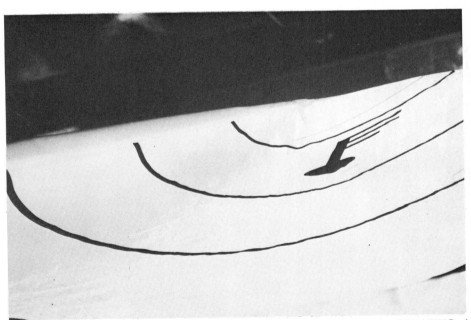

OVERTIGHTENING THE CUNNINGHAM PULLS THE DRAFT FORWARD, CREATING A LARGE, DEEP CURVE DIRECTLY BEHIND THE MAST AND, IN TURN, PREVENTING ONE FROM POINTING.

EASE THE OUTHAUL TO ADD DRAFT UNTIL YOU ARE SLIGHTLY OVERPOWERED.

AS MAINSHEET TENSION IS ADDED, THE MAST BENDS AND CUNNINGHAM AND OUTHAUL ADJUSTMENTS MUST BE ALTERED TO PROVIDE A POWERFUL SAIL.

WITHOUT A BOOM VANG, AS THE SAIL IS EASED THE BOOM CAN RIDE UP.

THE BOOM VANG SIMPLY HOLDS THE BOOM DOWN WHEN THE MAINSHEET NO LONGER CAN.

3 HIKING

Most of us think we know how to hike. Hiking is a simple matter of sticking your feet underneath the hiking strap or convenient cockpit lip and leaning over. However, there are a few tricks. Imagine, if you will, trying to support yourself in a half sit-up for half an hour. Somewhat of a chore, isn't it? Now imagine yourself in a reclined position with your knees elevated. You should be able to sit in this position considerably longer. A number of sailors have tried to build up their stomach muscles to support themselves for long periods of time, thinking that the further they get their bodies out of the boat, the more leverage they will have. While this might be true, the immobility of their position and the quickness with which they tire more than negates the advantage gained by this over-the-side hiking position.

The best hiking technique is one which places the body in what we call the "S" position. This means your body is like the letter "S" turned on its side. The hiking strap is between your toes and ankles and your knees are elevated above the deck. You are literally sitting on the side of the boat, not the deck. While in this position you will find you have good body control, as you can snap your body in and out and maintain good hand location. Your aft hand is in good position for accurate tiller response while your forward hand is in an excellant position for mainsheet and sail control adjustment. You can lean into your adjustments to provide maximum body effort into their control. This is a far cry from hiking out with your knees straight on the deck and leaning backwards, supporting all your weight with your stomach muscles.

Strength has really very little to do with the ability to hike for long periods of time. Just because you may be able to press two hundred pounds with one hand and do two hundred sit-ups at one time does not

FIGURE 14   WALL LEAN

mean that you will be able to hike out any longer than the next fellow. Hiking, because of its position and requirements, necessitates a non-movement type of strength. Proper hiking requires that you lock your legs in a position and hold them there. This can become rather difficult because as the muscles contract they start to shut off the flow of blood, causing a numbness and fatigue which eventually becomes quite uncomfortable. It is important to discipline your mind to overcome this numbness and its resultant **mental** fatigue so you will be able to stay over the side of the boat much longer.

An easy way to do this is to use an excercise which I will call the "wall lean" (Figure 14). To achieve the proper position, lean against a wall in a sitting position as if you were in a chair. Your back is flush against the wall, forming a right angle with your legs. Also your knees form a right angle. The longer you can hold this position, the longer you will be able to stay out over the side of the boat. In doing sit-ups or lifting weights you are constantly moving muscles and pumping new blood to them. Every movement refreshes them. In hiking you are supporting your weight for a long period without supplying new blood. It is important to overcome the numbness and mental fatigue that will slowly creep into your muscles and head.

You are probably thinking right now: "This is a great technique for getting body weight hung out over the side of the boat, but what do I do if the wind lets up or I should steer into the wind too much and the boat begins to luff? When the boat heels on top of me if I don't scramble back in, it will tip over on top of me." Curiously enough, just the opposite is true.

If you were to immediately scramble back into the boat the moment it heels on top of you, your entire weight would be located on the weather rail, thus helping push that side of the boat further down and accentuate the heel to windward. Instead, try this method. As the boat heels up on top of you, simply lean in against your knees. At the same time pull the tiller and the traveler control towards you. This will steer the boat away from the wind and oversheet the sail so that it heels the boat to leeward. Once this happens you can again ease the traveler control, straighten the tiller, and start sailing. This sounds very simple. Let's look into it a little further.

If you stay in a hiked position when the boat heels to windward, the moment you become immersed in the water you lose all your hiking power because your body becomes bouyant. This bouyancy would immediately stop the boat from heeling to windward. However, if you try to get into the boat from this position, it will topple over on top of you. It is interesting to try this at the dock and make a few bets with your fellow skippers. You will find that even a boat with a trapeze cannot be tipped over as long as the crew is in the water. But the moment they try to raise themselves from the water or pull on the boat with their feet, it will tip over on top of them. Once you clear the water you are at your maximum hiking position, as not only is your body wet and heavy, but at that moment you have the most leverage on the sail.

With boats that have a mainsheet but no traveler control, the same technique works. As the boat heels over on top of you, again lay against your knees and immediately pull the tiller *and* mainsheet. This oversheets the sail and steers the boat away from the wind. In both types of boats, steering the boat away from the wind and oversheeting the sail are the keys to the correction of heeling to windward.

4 HEAVY WEATHER

In heavy weather all the techniques we have been discussing come into play. When the wind is up, you have more than enough power to make your boat go fast. The situation is reversed, and the problem becomes how to eliminate power. The goal is to spill off power so that the boat becomes both more manageable and more efficient.

The first method of eliminating power is to flatten the sail. Tightening the outhaul will accomplish this goal. But more can be done. Tightening the cunningham will pull the draft forward. Remember that most of the sail's cloth is located along the **leech** and has a tendency to stretch more. Tightening the cunningham will move the draft forward and help reduce the weather helm developed when sail draft is too far aft. Finally, pull in the mainsheet. This will bend the mast and flatten the sail. If you are still overpowered, ease the traveler to leeward. This will begin to spill air. Once these adjustments are made, simply steer the boat through the waves, keep the sail full and the boat driving forward.

However, if you still find yourself overpowered with this type of adjustment, ease the mainsheet. The easing of the mainsheet initially allows the boom to move straight up, which in turn allows the leech to twist and spill air out of the sail. You can look at this adjustment as **feathering** the sail, and is important to remember because you can almost instantaneously eliminate all the power of the sail.

There is one more technique to remember. That is to lock the mainsheet traveler amidships and make your mainsheet adjustments from that position. This allows the sail leech to twist to leeward and permits you to point much closer to the wind. This proves to be a big advantage as you begin to combine the best two possible worlds -- the instantaneous reduction of power and the ability to point close to the wind.

With the boat which does not have a mid-boom traveler mainsheet system, it is important to be able to trim the sail correctly and induce a leech twist as quickly as possible in overpowering gusts. This can be done by simply maintaining your "S" position. Keep the boat driving to windward by filling the sail in the lulls between the gusts. As the gust approaches, drive slightly to leeward to gain speed, then slowly round up into the gust with lots of speed. You will find as soon as you round into the gust you can sheet in and the boat will accelerate through the gust.

5 TACKING

Most people make one common mistake when they tack. They simply tack. They throw the tiller hard to leeward, let the boat round up, and follow the tiller across to the other side of the boat. This is an extremely slow way of tacking because for most of the turn the boat is simply not sailing -- it is coasting around on the momentum it had gained before the tack was initiated. When one completes a tack in this manner the boat is at a dead stop and must regain all its lost speed and momentum.

A far better method of tacking is called the **roll tack**. The roll tack is simply a method which allows the boat to sail itself through the entire turn. Let's assume you are ready to tack. Follow this procedure: put the tiller to leeward, hike out as far as possible to heel the boat to windward, and let go of the tiller; as the boat passes through the eye of the wind, move quickly to the new windward side and hike out. As the boat levels off it will be accelerating onto the new tack, and you will have successfully completed the roll tack.

This sounds rather too easy, so let's investigate the roll tack a little further by running through it again in greater depth. As you are ready to tack, start the tiller leeward. Normally this will mean only a six to ten inch tiller movement because in a roll tack it is not necessary to push the tiller a great distance, or to hold on to the tiller once the turn is initiated. Then hike out as far as possible. This will heel the boat to windward. By doing so three things happen. First, you place the area of the hull which is on the inside of the turn in the water and lift the area of the hull which is on the outside of the turn clear of the water. Also, you lift the fore and aft ends of the hull. The boat literally pivots about the spot you are sitting. Second, as the boat heels to windward, the motion of heeling to windward fills the sail with air, driving the boat forward. Third, as the boat heels to windward the board makes a sweep through the water and sculls the boat forward.

As the boat reaches head to wind, dive across the cockpit to the new windward side and immediately get into a hiked position. This will reverse the heel. As this motion occurs, the board swings back to a vertical position, sculling the boat forward. Simultaneously the sail moves through an arc back to a vertical position, filling and propelling the boat forward. Once the boat begins to accelerate onto a new tack, you can look back and see the tiller centering itself. Allowing the rudder blade to center itself causes less drag through the tack. Simply grab the tiller as it goes by.

Here are some hints to help make the roll tack easier. First, as you round into the wind, it is helpful to pull in the sail with either the mainsheet or the traveler control. This keeps the sail driving for a longer period of time. Once into the wind, however, it is a good idea to ease the sail for the new tack so that the boat will turn away from the wind and accelerate more quickly. Second, there is alot of discussion as to which way you should face when tacking. Many people suggest always looking forward so you know what is going to happen. My attitude is that whether you face forward or aft is immaterial. It is far more important to coordinate your efforts with the boat, getting the boat from one tack to another as quickly, smartly, smoothly and fast as possible. If you have a crew, it is important to coordinate your efforts and facing positions so that you don't bump into each other and destroy the efficiency of the roll tack.

A review of the roll tack demonstrates it as a useful, efficient tool in racing, particularly when tacking in light to medium air and in relatively smooth or flat seas. But what happens when the wind picks up and the sea is running? It is fairly obvious that a roll tack is not going to be quite as easy and efficient. No longer will you be able to tack at will. Rather, your tack must be planned in advance.

When the wind is up and there is wave motion, most people tend to slam the boat through the tack. When they get ready to tack, they ease away from the wind slightly to gain speed, then throw up the tiller hard to leeward and pray that they don't come to a dead stop into the wind. And more than likely they do! The problem is that the turn was not planned to the wave motion. As they begin their turn, they have steered straight into the oncoming wave, which knocks them backwards rather than allowing them to complete the turn. This loss of forward speed will stop them head to wind, and they end up in **irons**. We all have had this happen to us at one time or another. To alleviate the problem many people will steer further away from the wind, gain even more speed, and then attempt to make the turn from almost a reaching position. But this can also easily result in failure.

In high wind and wave conditions it is important to remember to **time yourself to the motion of the waves**. Let's take the easiest way first. Look for a relatively smooth area of water to tack in, where the wave pattern has broken down. As the boat enters this flat area of water, simply put the tiller to leeward a little more violently than you would on a normal roll tack. Go through the roll tack drill, only don't remain on the old windward side quite as long. You will find that as the boat rounds into the wind, the flat area in which you were making your turn will have disappeared and the next set of waves will knock the bow on to its new tack. You can see from this maneuver that again we have allowed the boat to sail itself, letting the wind and the water do all the work.

The second method of tacking in these conditions calls for timing your turn to the rhythm of the waves. The same rules apply -- let the wind and waves do the work for you. We want the boat to head to wind in such a position that as it passes through head to wind, the next wave or set of waves will knock the bow on to the new tack. It will take practice, as it's all too easy to steer the boat into a position where it gets hit by a wave and knocked straight into irons.

In heavy air and high sea conditions one should steer into the wind up the face of a wave, and away from the wind down the back side of a wave. The reason for this is quite simple: as you are rising on the wave more and more sail is becoming exposed to the wind and it becomes progressively difficult to hold the boat down; steering away from the wind down the back-side of a wave allows you to accelerate in the lighter air conditions of the wave trough. Do not initiate your turn until you are on the very crest of the wave. This allows you to roll tack as the wave passes by the transom of the boat. The offset rudder will literally kick the transom around and push the bow towards its new tack. The next oncoming wave will accentuate this turn and allow you to accelerate on to the new tack.

Tacking in heavy weather is a difficult technique to learn, but once mastered it becomes a devastating tool. You will be accelerating and sailing while many of your competitors will be caught head to wind or laboring with the always slow methods of getting out of irons.

I should point out that many times while you are attempting to roll tack, the boat for some reason might stall just as you get beyond head to wind, and appear to you as though you have missed the tack. This is generally a result of poorly coordinating your roll tack with either the wind and waves or the mechanics of the roll tack itself. There is an easy and quick technique to get out of this condition, provided the boat has not come to a dead stop. Grasp the boom with your forward hand and snap it sharply to windward; at the same time, steer away from the wind with the tiller. This quick motion will force the bow onto the new tack and allow you to sail on with little loss of time and distance. It is important to practice this technique. You never know when a disastrous tack may strike.

lift the daggerboard, the boat will have shimmed slightly, unloading the board pressure and allowing you to pull it up with considerable ease. Always lift the board. Remember, the simple action of grasping the board will tend to generate not only fore and aft motion, but side to side motion, and could cause difficulty in lifting the board. Your attempt to raise the board may only jam it in its trunk. Place your hand under either the finger grips or lifting handle, and lift with your fingertips, carefully avoiding any extraneous motions or forces.

Now the question is, "How high do you raise the board while reaching?" It is best to raise the board too high. This will generate side slipping and you will feel the resultant weather helm. Get into a hiked "S" position and allow the boat to accelerate. Then slowly start tapping the daggerboard down, either with your forward hand or foot, until you feel the helm become almost neutral. If you push the daggerboard too far down you will immediately notice an increase of weather helm as the boat begins to heel to leeward and pivot around the extended daggerboard.

You can see that daggerboard adjustment is quite critical to hull trim, weather helm and boat speed. Adjustment of the board is not a magic half-way placement, but rather an adjustment which is made to a given reach, under given wind conditions. The closer the reach, the more board you must have extended; the broader the reach or the more you approach a run, the more board you may retract.

There are several other things that should be considered while reaching. The technique of **shimming** the boat to raise the board will work on virtually every boat with a moveable centerboard. It doesn't matter if you have a daggerboard, a centerboard, or even a leeboard. This technique will work. Practice this adjustment technique. Practice is the only way you can determine the proper adjustment for the board and feel the changes in the weather helm. With very little practice you will soon know where to set the daggerboard correctly. I repeat, board adjustment is probably the most overlooked adjustment in small boat racing, yet is probably the simplest, easiest adjustment one can learn and enjoy.

As a quick review of what happens on a reaching leg, let's start from rounding the weather mark. After rounding the mark, getting the boat set up is somewhat of a Chinese fire drill. Each of us will have to determine the best order to make the necessary adjustments. Remember the following: ease the cunningham and outhaul, ease the traveler control, raise and adjust the daggerboard, and ease the mainsheet. Once these adjustments have been made, skipper and crew adjustments must be taken care of. Keep the boat flat from side to side, move your weight aft as the boat accelerates. Get the boat planing. As the apparent wind moves forward, either sheet in and/or bear away to stay in the gust. If the boat begins to decelerate, fall off the plane, and as the apparent wind begins to move aft, slowly round into the wind and ease the sail. Most important, keep the boat moving as fast as possible during the entire reaching leg.

It is easy to recognize the advantage of all these adjustments when you look at the guy who merely eases his sail out, pulls his daggerboard half way up, and sits in his boat waiting for the wind and waves to effect him. He is totally at the mercy of the elements. He only accelerates when a gust hits him and stays with him. And because his daggerboard may not be adjusted correctly, he may not use that gust to its ultimate advantage. But with constant adjustments you are continually attacking the course, attacking the elements, continually adjusting the sail, the daggerboard, and yourself in relationship to the boat. Even if you miss a gust or fall off the plane, you know what has happened and you can make the quick adjustments that will reestablish the boat planing and moving as quickly as possible. The fellow who sits back and relaxes will not only fail to realize what has happened, but will lose valuable time and distance as he waits for the next gust to hit him and propel him forward.

7 RUNNING

Running is the next area for discussion. As in reaching, most people refer to running as a coasting leg of the course. They merely let the sail all the way out, sit back, relax, and seem totally willing to allow the elements to control their destiny. As in reaching, one must **attack** the running leg of the course. Let's first make the necessary adjustments to the boat.

Running is a further extension of off wind sailing, and by its nature calls for the development of as much power as possible. This generally means further easing the cunningham and outhaul so that the sail begins to take a spinnaker-like or pressure pocket appearance. If you adjust the sail and get large diagonal wrinkles or folds across the sail, it is probably best to tighten the cunningham and outhaul to remove them. For both reaching and running, if the sail looks powerful with the absence of large wrinkles and creases, it is powerful. Next, ease the traveler control all the way to leeward and ease the sail to its furthest extent.

There is one piece of equipment which becomes quite important at this stage. We have not discussed the purpose of the **boom vang** until now because it interferes with your sail adjustments upwind. As you are sailing upwind, mainsheet tension controls the height of the boom off the deck, which in turn controls not only the mast bend, but leech tension, and in combination with the cunningham and outhaul gives you your sail shape. However, as you begin to sail on a reach or run, the boom is no longer over the traveler. If the boom was unrestricted, it would not only go out, but up. The sail would then begin to twist excessively and you would loose power.

With a mid-boom sheeted boat, for certain points of sailing, such as close reaching, you can allow the traveler to slide to leeward and thereby align the traveler blocks directly under the boom. This retains your up and down boom control and still allows you to ease the sail to leeward.

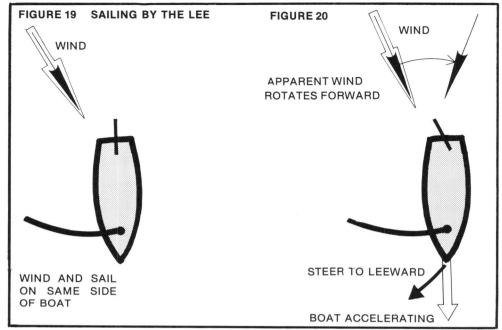

FIGURE 19 SAILING BY THE LEE

FIGURE 20

WIND

WIND

APPARENT WIND
ROTATES FORWARD

WIND AND SAIL
ON SAME SIDE
OF BOAT

STEER TO LEEWARD

BOAT ACCELERATING

However, once you have reached the end of the traveler, further easing of the mainsheet allows the boom to rise, inducing extensive leech twisting and loss of power. The boom vang simply prevents the boom from rising, but does not prohibit any side to side motion.

There are very few boom vangs in existence which allow any easy adjustment once the sail has been eased for reaching and running. Therefore, the boom vang must be set properly before easing the sail. Just before you arrive at the weather mark, pull the boom vang in until it is taking part of the load of the mainsheet, thereby matching the boom height, mast bend and leech tension that you set up while beating. The boom vang will hold that relationship for either reaching or running. Since you have already set your mainsheet tension for the given conditions, it is advantageous to maintain that tension for off wind sailing as well.

As in reaching, you will find the boat will try to plane. Attempt to keep the boat more or less flat, side to side, moving your weight fore and aft as you attempt to nurse it onto a plane. You will find that as each successive gust comes the boat will rapidly accelerate and decelerate. During these accelerations and decelerations, the apparent wind will move considerably. As a boat accelerates the apparent wind will move forward, allowing you to **sail by the lee** slightly. **Sailing by the lee** means that the wind and sail are on the same side of the boat (Figure 19 & 20). However, as the boat decelerates, the wind will slowly rotate aft. When this happens, you must steer slightly to windward to prevent an accidental jibe (Figure 21).

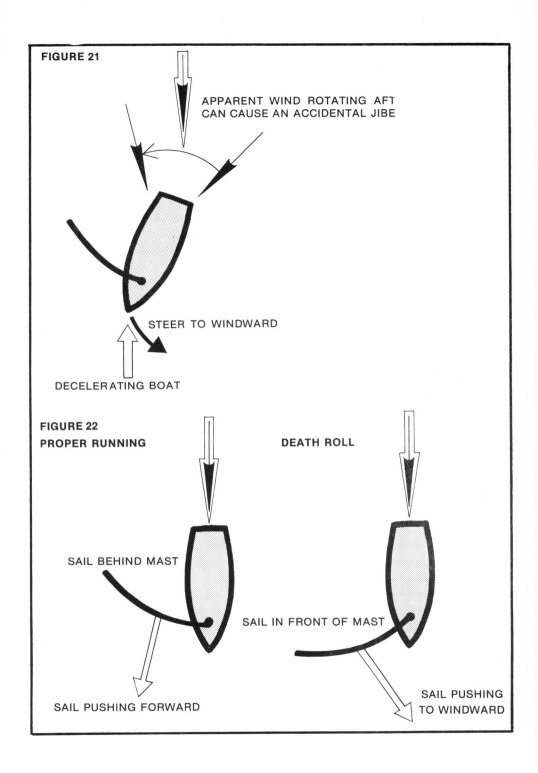

FIGURE 21

APPARENT WIND ROTATING AFT
CAN CAUSE AN ACCIDENTAL JIBE

STEER TO WINDWARD

DECELERATING BOAT

FIGURE 22
PROPER RUNNING

DEATH ROLL

SAIL BEHIND MAST

SAIL IN FRONT OF MAST

SAIL PUSHING FORWARD

SAIL PUSHING
TO WINDWARD

It is important to be alert to the phenomenon known as the **death roll**. This occurs while running, and is caused when the sail moves forward of the mast. The sail is no longer pushing the boat forward, but rather is pushing it to windward (Figure 22). The boat then rolls violently to windward with the sail high in the air. To counteract this motion you dive across the boat to get to the high leeward side. When you do so, the boat reacts by violently rolling to leeward, many times plunging the end of the boom into the water. To counteract this quick motion, you again jump to the weather side, and the boat rolls quickly over on top of you.

A death roll is generally a one, two, three motion -- on three you capsize to weather. This wild motion can be corrected by simply pulling in the sail. Most people believe that the boom reflects the plane of the sail, but with loose footed sails or rigs without stays, this may not be so. The sail will fill out in front of the boom and therefore be quite a distance from the boom itself. Pulling in the mainsheet will replace the sail in its forward driving position, eliminating the side thrust generated when it fills ahead of the mast.

Even when sailing a boat with shrouds, it is possible for the sail to get in front of the mast. This happens when the boom vang is not set and the "boom climbs the shroud." This climbing allows the sail to fold at the leech and twist past the mast. The boat reacts to this poor seamanship by death rolling. To avoid this disaster, it is important to not only pull in the sail but to properly tighten the boom vang.

There are a couple of techniques you will find helpful while running. First, bypass as many parts of the mainsheet as possible so you have more direct and positive control of the sail. This allows rapid adjustment for acceleration and deceleration in gusts, and also gives you the ability of snapping in the sail should you begin to death roll. If you find bypassing the mainsheet system too difficult and the boat begins to death roll, simply grab all the parts of the mainsheet system and pull for all you're worth. Second, practice recovery from a death roll by sailing on a medium air day and easing the sail to a point where you know you will begin to death roll. As you roll, practice snapping in the sail by either a rapid mainsheet adjustment or by pulling all the parts of the mainsheet system. You will find that although the boat is heeled to weather it will accelerate very rapidly and begin to plane. It is almost like "pumping" the boat forward.

In heavier air, you will find it useful to oversheet. Pull the boom and sail in to a point where the sail is less than 90 degrees to the mast. This will reduce the tendency of the boat to death roll and reduce some of the exposed area of the sail to the wind. To eliminate some drive and death roll tendencies, you may find yourself oversheeting to the point where the boom is only 60 to 70 degrees to the centerline of the boat (Figure 23).

In most conditions it is helpful to heel the boat slightly to windward. The reason is simple. If you were to leave the boat flat in the water, the

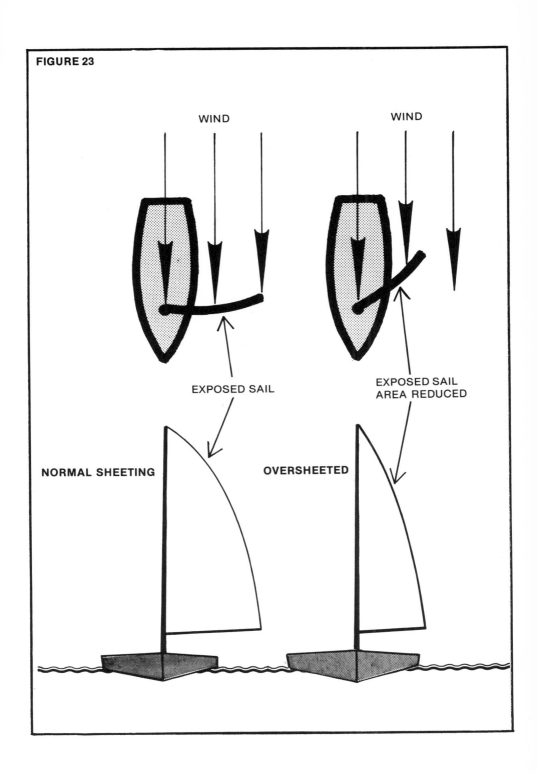

FIGURE 23

WIND

WIND

EXPOSED SAIL

EXPOSED SAIL
AREA REDUCED

NORMAL SHEETING

OVERSHEETED

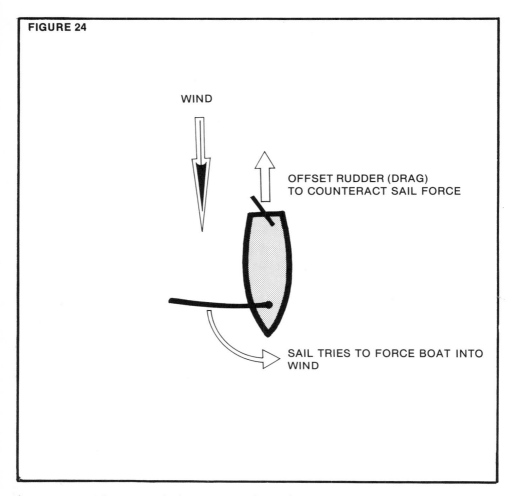

FIGURE 24

WIND

OFFSET RUDDER (DRAG)
TO COUNTERACT SAIL FORCE

SAIL TRIES TO FORCE BOAT INTO
WIND

boom would be extended over one side of the boat, and the sail (which is on that side of the boat) would tend to drive or twist the boat into the wind. In other words, one side of the boat (the side with the sail) is trying to pass the other side of the boat. To counteract this turning motion, pull the tiller slightly to windward. This offsets the rudder and sails the boat straight again. However, the offset rudder blade creates considerable drag (Figure 24). To remove this drag, heel the boat to windward and move the center of effort of the sail over the center of motion of the boat. When the two line up, the boat will go straight ahead and the rudder can be centered. By heeling the boat more to windward, the center of effort of the sail crosses over the center of motion of the boat and the boat will steer itself to leeward. By letting the boat heel slightly to leeward, the center of effort of the sail crosses back to its original side and the boat will begin to steer itself into the wind. It is easier to steer the boat to windward than to leeward. (Figure 25, 26 & 27).

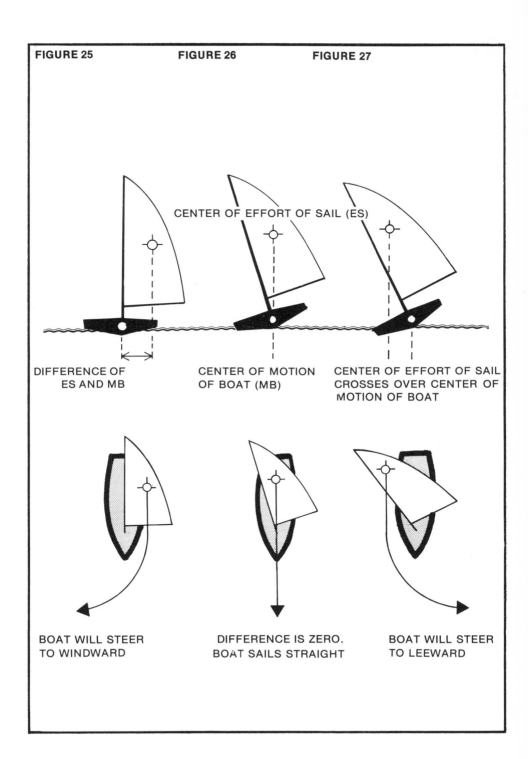

FIGURE 25   **FIGURE 26**   **FIGURE 27**

CENTER OF EFFORT OF SAIL (ES)

DIFFERENCE OF
ES AND MB

CENTER OF MOTION
OF BOAT (MB)

CENTER OF EFFORT OF SAIL
CROSSES OVER CENTER OF
MOTION OF BOAT

BOAT WILL STEER
TO WINDWARD

DIFFERENCE IS ZERO.
BOAT SAILS STRAIGHT

BOAT WILL STEER
TO LEEWARD

SAIL WITH THE HULL UNDER THE SAIL WHEN RUNNING. HEEL THE BOAT TO WEATHER TO ELIMINATE WEATHER HELM. BY HEELING BACK AND FORTH YOU CAN STEER DOWNWIND WITHOUT THE RUDDER.

You now have a method for steering the boat downwind without using the tiller, as you induce the boat to go the direction you want by heeling the boat. This technique can be used to devastating advantage. With practice, you will eventually be able to go downwind in lighter air with the rudder blade raised.

This technique works well when using a spinnaker or winging out the jib. The exposed sail area on each side of the mast is about equal and therefore almost balances the helm. When you heel the boat from one side to the other, considerably less heel will induce a turn.

In most cases when running, the board can be raised to its fullest extent. You will find it helpful, however, to leave just the tip of the board exposed from the bottom of the hull. This gives you some directional control so the boat can be steered more easily and also gives a slight amount of lateral resistance to prevent easy side to side rolling.

Another reason to leave the board slightly down is to fill the trunk. In most daggerboard boats there are no trunk flaps to seal off the end of the daggerboard trunk. By leaving the daggerboard slightly down you fill the slot and prevent water from circulating in the bottom of the trunk. This reduces drag. On most centerboard boats there are trunk flaps or gaskets which seal off the end of the trunk. By leaving the board slightly down, you reduce the tendency of the flaps to bend with the waves.

8 JIBING

The maneuver that causes most people the most trouble is **jibing**. A **jibe** is a difficult maneuver to complete efficiently because it is accomplished by steering away from the wind with full power on. Let's discuss a correct jibe, and then cover the areas where most people have trouble.

To jibe correctly, steer away from the wind slightly (a very shallow turn), and at the same time quickly pull in the sail. This will cause your jibe to occur sooner and give you some control over the movement of the boom and sail. As the sail snaps across the boat and fills on the new tack, straighten the tiller and ease the sheet through your hands. You have thus successfully completed a jibe. The key is pulling in the sail in combination with a shallow turn (Figure 28).

To jibe with a mid-boom sheeted boat, simply steer away from the wind, grab all the parts of the mainsheet and literally throw the sail from one side of the boat to the other. This completes the jibe quickly and much more efficiently, as you are now sailing on the new tack almost twice as fast as if you were to pull in the mainsheet from its tail.

The trouble most people have jibing down wind is steering the boat without pulling in on the mainsheet. They continue to sail further and further by the lee until finally the wind is able to get to the leeward side of the sail and throw it uncontrollably from one side of the boat to the other. When this happens, the boat is pointed on a broad reach, but the sail is eased for a run and simply flutters in the wind with the boat dead in the water. It is then necessary to steer away from the wind and return to the course required to fill the sail. You can see how this is a very inefficient method (Figure 29).

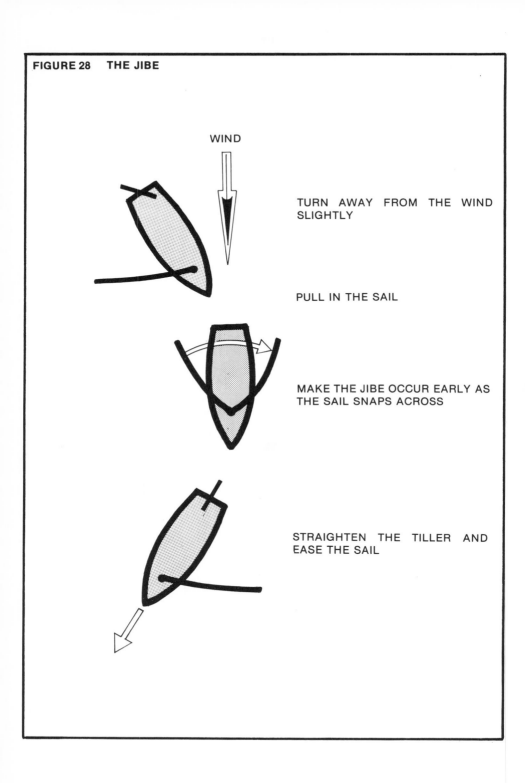

FIGURE 28   THE JIBE

WIND

TURN AWAY FROM THE WIND SLIGHTLY

PULL IN THE SAIL

MAKE THE JIBE OCCUR EARLY AS THE SAIL SNAPS ACROSS

STRAIGHTEN THE TILLER AND EASE THE SAIL

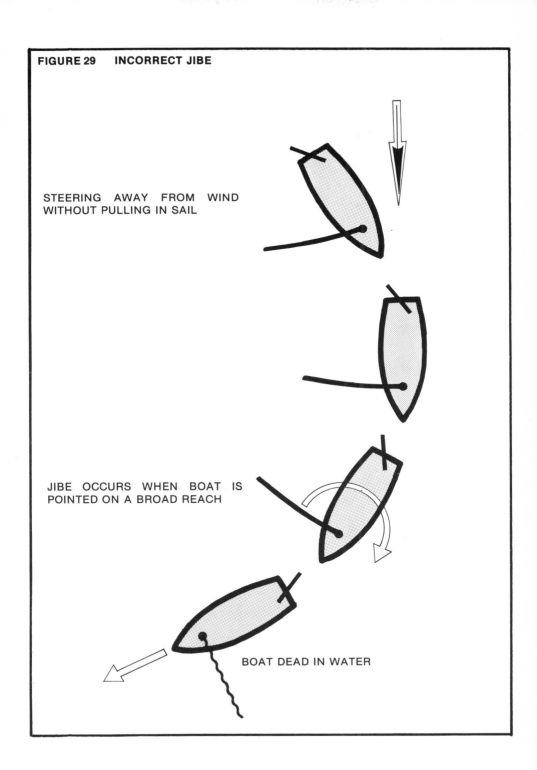

FIGURE 29   INCORRECT JIBE

STEERING AWAY FROM WIND
WITHOUT PULLING IN SAIL

JIBE OCCURS WHEN BOAT IS
POINTED ON A BROAD REACH

BOAT DEAD IN WATER

It is important to point out that jibing should not be completed in the lulls between gusts, but rather while accelerating in a gust. The reason is clear. If you wait for the gust to pass and attempt your jibe, you will find that by the time you have completed it, the next gust will hit you. Your boat's speed is almost nonexistent and you get the full force of the gust to contend with. However, if you attempt your jibe while accelerating in a gust, you will find that when your boat has reached its maximum speed, the apparent wind (the wind you feel pushing) will become very light. As you complete your jibe, the strongest force of the gust will have passed you. You will be going faster than the wind around you, thus relieving the violence of the jibe. The faster the boat is moving, the lighter the wind during the jibe, and the less violent the jibe. This technique makes it very easy to control your jibe.

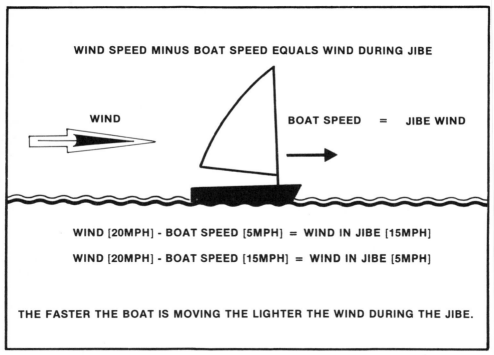

WIND SPEED MINUS BOAT SPEED EQUALS WIND DURING JIBE

WIND

BOAT SPEED = JIBE WIND

WIND [20MPH] - BOAT SPEED [5MPH] = WIND IN JIBE [15MPH]

WIND [20MPH] - BOAT SPEED [15MPH] = WIND IN JIBE [5MPH]

THE FASTER THE BOAT IS MOVING THE LIGHTER THE WIND DURING THE JIBE.

Another hint for jibing in heavy weather is to pull in as much sheet as possible with one draw of your arm, and then cleat the sheet. By doing this, the next movement of either grabbing all the parts of the mainsheet or pulling the mainsheet itself will become much more efficient. As the jibe is completed, the sail will not go out to its fullest extent. The oversheeted sail will prevent death rolling on the new tack.

Jibing is more complicated with a spinnaker or winged jib. It is best to jibe the mainsail first, allowing the skipper and crew to concentrate on one sail at a time. Once the main is jibed, the spinnaker or jib can be jibed with the skipper in a position to help the crew. It is important to have a set procedure for jibing. If you don't you'll find your jibes slow, confusing and costly. Skipper and crew should constantly communicate. Each should tell the other how to improve his jibing technique, and once you have a procedure, practice it until it is second nature.

Board position is also critical while jibing. It is best to have the board in a raised position while jibing. With an extended board it is more difficult to steer the boat away from the wind to initiate the jibe and, as the jibe is completed, the boat will pivot around the extended board, swinging violently to windward. When this occurs, you try to correct the violent motion by steering to leeward, which only complicates matters, as the boat will heel wildly to leeward. This phenomenon is known as **tripping over the board**.

By having the board in a raised position, you will find that it is easier to steer the boat away from the wind because the bow of the boat will easily slide to leeward, and as the sail snaps full on the new tack, the boat will literally slide sideways, maintaining its new course.

Jibing from one reach to another reach is a different maneuver. In light air, most people don't have any trouble because they can simply overpower the boat with the rudder. They can steer around the reaching mark, jibe the sail and get going on the new reach with very little difficulty. However, as the wind increases, so does the difficulty of the jibe. We have all seen some extremely wild jibes and capsizes around the reaching mark, what we call the "demolition derby" at the reaching mark. This fiasco is started by someone who has lost control of his boat while attempting to jibe around the reaching mark, and in so doing, involves other sailors who are not expecting his circus act.

The technique for jibing around a reach mark is fairly similar to that of a jibe completed on a run. However, there are some exceptions and additional techniques. As you attempt your jibe and begin to bear off, ease the sail out. In bearing off you start to approach a run, therefore the sail should be set in that position. Keeping the sail in makes it difficult to bear off. The sail will continue to drive you forward, not to leeward. However, once pointed downwind, retrieve as much sheet at possible. Continue your turn and sheet retrieval until the sail snaps over the boat. The moment the sail snaps across, straighten the tiller. This will straighten your course. Now quickly ease the sail on a new tack and allow the boat to accelerate, even though you may not be pointing directly towards the next mark. Once the boat accelerates on the new tack, aim it towards the next mark and begin to adjust the sheet (Figure 30).

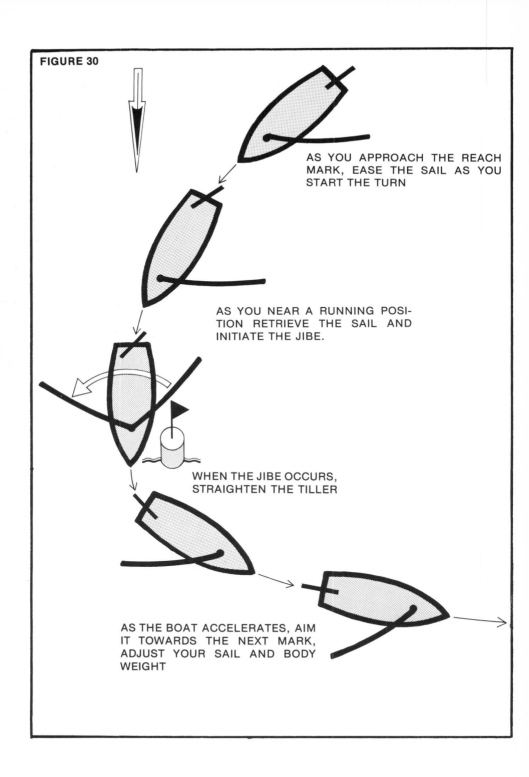

FIGURE 30

AS YOU APPROACH THE REACH MARK, EASE THE SAIL AS YOU START THE TURN

AS YOU NEAR A RUNNING POSITION RETRIEVE THE SAIL AND INITIATE THE JIBE.

WHEN THE JIBE OCCURS, STRAIGHTEN THE TILLER

AS THE BOAT ACCELERATES, AIM IT TOWARDS THE NEXT MARK, ADJUST YOUR SAIL AND BODY WEIGHT

The same techniques of grabbing all parts of the mainsheet, pulling one full draw of sheet and making your turn as shallow as possible apply on a reach to reach jibe, especially in heavy weather. In heavy weather, making your turn too sharp will result in a capsize because of the speed of the jibe and the centrifugal force of the turn. You will find in heavy weather it is possible to turn so violently that the boat falls to the outside of the turn. When the jibe finally occurs, the sail literally pushes the boat over.

One question that might be on your mind is, "How do I get from one side of the boat to the other? Should I be pointed forward or aft? Should I be handling the tiller with my right hand or my left hand?" Again, my attitude is that whether you face forward or aft is immaterial. Each sailor must decide what is the easiest, most efficient and direct for him. The idea of facing forward so that you will know what you are running into is good, but if you are in the middle of a jibe and you don't know in advance you are going to hit a boat, it is too late to do anything about it. Any maneuver should have been done well in advance of a collision. If you are hell bent on a collision course, it might be better to be facing aft. At least you won't see your boat impale another. But seriously, whether you face forward or aft, your jibing technique must become a habit. If you change your technique every time you jibe you will never develop a smooth, efficient procedure.

A HOBIE-16 ABOUT TO GO OVER IN HIGH SEAS.

9 CAPSIZING

Most people don't practice capsizing. They feel that it is an indignity to capsize in a race, and, if they do capsize, God must be punishing them for something. Yet a capsize is part of the sailing game, especially in small, high performance boats. A capsize is not something to be feared or to be made light of, but rather an item that must be practiced. The reason is straight forward. Practice will teach you when a capsize is imminent, and thus you can avoid it. If you capsize three times on a reach, don't know why, and don't try to correct it, these capsizes are useless to your learning process and you'll continue to capsize in similar conditions. There is no rule that says once you have capsized you are not allowed to continue racing. For that matter, you can still win the race. Therefore it is important to practice capsizing so you will know what causes a capsize and what to do with yourself once it has occured.

When a capsize does occur, most people fall off the boat between the hull and the boom. Then they either dive underneath or swim around the end of the overturned hull and grab the board from the bottom side. This is a very slow method of righting the boat. The following technique will save time, effort and your wrist watch. When the boat capsizes to leeward, hold on to the high side until the mast hits the water. Then step down on the boom. Quickly walk along the boom to the mast, step on the mast, and then over the side onto the board. You will find that you are on the board far more quickly, far more efficiently than you had ever thought possible. With a little practice you will be able to right the boat without falling into the water and be on the board, ready to sail even as the sail is still emerging from the surface of the water. Keep one thing in mind however. When walking along the boom and mast, **step lively**. The longer you take, the more the top of the mast will dip below the surface of the water.

10 CONCLUSION AT MID-COURSE

The techniques we have introduced are developed not only for speed, but ease in boat handling. You will find that your boat sails itself faster than you can. Once you have the sail producing the power you can use efficiently and get the hull and sail trimmed to the point where the helm is reduced to its minimum, you can almost sit on the boat and let it do all the work.

I have tried to show little tricks and techniques which take advantage of every change in the dynamic exchange between boat, wind and water. By adjusting the cunningham, outhaul and mainsheet you can get the most out of your sail and rig for any given condition. The final and ultimate adjustments on your boat must be those you make, geared to your own style of sailing.

To master these techniques, practice them before each race. Spend the first three or four weekends of your racing season getting to the club early and sailing two to three hours before each race. Practice in a highly concentrated effort those techniques you feel need to be developed and refined. In a short time you will become more comfortable in your boat, with these techniques becoming a natural part of your style of sailing. Only then can they become a weapon you can effectively use in racing.

The winner of a race doesn't usually make one tactical decision that puts him a half mile ahead of the fleet. He does a number of small things throughout the race to sail his boat more effectively and efficiently than those around him. People that are winning are literally sailing their boat more efficiently than those people behind. Surely tactical decisions come into play, but tactical decisions are based on what is happening for the given conditions. You only have time to make smart tactical decisions once you have the basics down pat. The more efficiently you sail your boat, the easier it becomes to make tactical decisions.

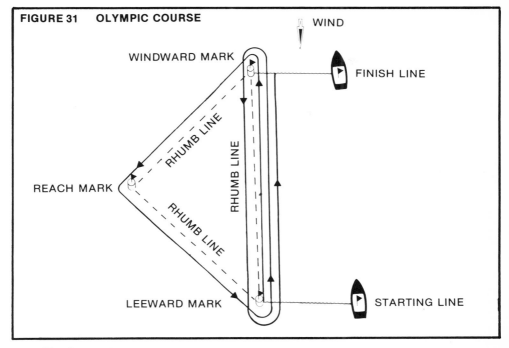

FIGURE 31   OLYMPIC COURSE

WIND

WINDWARD MARK

FINISH LINE

RHUMB LINE

RHUMB LINE

RHUMB LINE

REACH MARK

RHUMB LINE

LEEWARD MARK

STARTING LINE

To this point we have discussed a number of techniques which you can use to make your boat move through the water most quickly for the given conditions. The fast sailors have developed these techniques into devastating skills. Everything from sail adjustment to roll tacking are second nature. They literally feel when their boat is not sailing fastest and make steps to correct the condition immediately.

In the next section of this book I will discuss additional techniques which allow the fast sailor to use his boat in the most efficient manner on the race course. I will discuss these techniques by sailing an imaginary race around a Olympic course, which consists of a beat, reach, reach, beat, run and a final beat to the finish (Figure 31). Remember at all times during this race that the skills we discussed earlier must be used. It is impossible to win races on tactics and strategy alone. If you can't make your boat develop its full potential for the given conditions it will be easy for someone who can to sail his boat past you, even with poor starts and bad tactics. Strategy and tactics only allow you to make up for minor mistakes and can only be used when your boat is being sailed efficiently.

We will start our next discussion with the wind. All of us know that it is the wind which makes our boats move. In the first section we discussed how to make our boat sail efficiently in all wind conditions. Now we discuss specific wind conditions, how they effect your boat and how to predict their changes. From there we will discuss starting techniques and then sail our imaginary olympic race course.

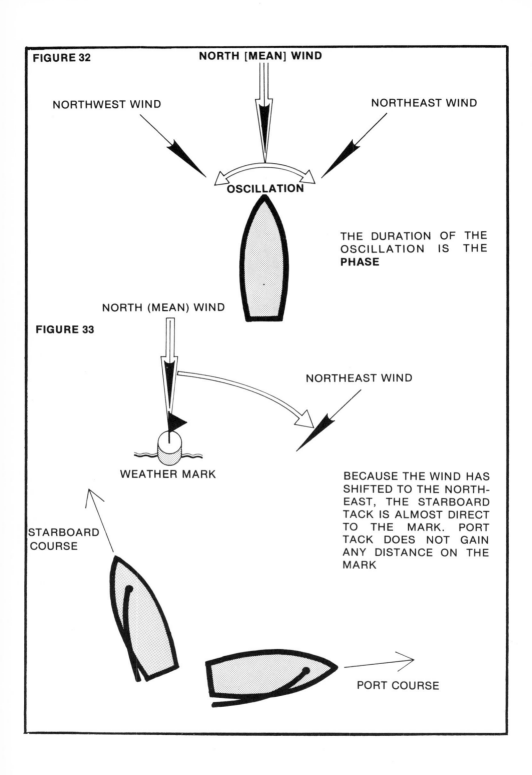

FIGURE 32

NORTH [MEAN] WIND

NORTHWEST WIND

NORTHEAST WIND

OSCILLATION

THE DURATION OF THE OSCILLATION IS THE **PHASE**

NORTH (MEAN) WIND

FIGURE 33

NORTHEAST WIND

WEATHER MARK

BECAUSE THE WIND HAS SHIFTED TO THE NORTH-EAST, THE STARBOARD TACK IS ALMOST DIRECT TO THE MARK. PORT TACK DOES NOT GAIN ANY DISTANCE ON THE MARK

STARBOARD COURSE

PORT COURSE

11 THE WIND

The wind does not blow in one given direction at one given speed -- it fluctuates in direction and velocity, and these fluctuations can be very great or very subtle. As such, they are one of the major variables in boat racing. The fast sailor, needless to say, takes advantage of these fluctuations.

In discussing the wind, we talk about **normal wind** or **mean wind** and its shifts. For the moment, let's discuss wind shifts and then we will give everything a name. We have all heard the weather man say, "The wind is from the north at 15-17 miles an hour." The wind he is discussing is not a steady wind that blows directly from the north and exactly at 15-17 miles an hour. He is announcing average conditions. In reality, you will find that the wind is blowing from both slightly west of north and slightly east of north most of the time, and is fluctuating anywhere from ten to twenty miles an hour.

The wind is affected by the heat of the land, heat of the water, and the objects it must go around. Most winds have what we call an **oscillation**. Oscillation simply means that the wind blows from one side or the other of a given direction (mean) for roughly an equal amount of time (a phase that the wind goes through). Example: the wind is blowing northwest for two minutes, and then back to north for a minute. Thus the wind rotates through what we call an **oscillational phase** -- a very complicated term for shifting wind (Figure 32).

A good race course starts with a beat to windward. The race committee will attempt to average out the wind shifts so that from the starting line the weather mark is directly into the mean wind. The racer must pick the shortest distance or route from the starting line to this weather mark, and to do so, must take advantage of the wind shifts. As an example, let's use a north wind and two boats.

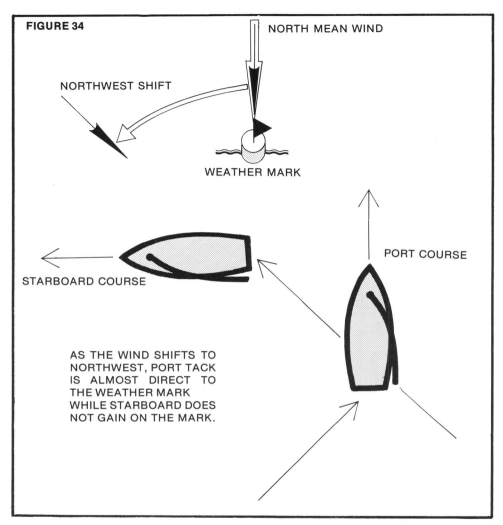

FIGURE 34

NORTH MEAN WIND

NORTHWEST SHIFT

WEATHER MARK

PORT COURSE

STARBOARD COURSE

AS THE WIND SHIFTS TO NORTHWEST, PORT TACK IS ALMOST DIRECT TO THE WEATHER MARK WHILE STARBOARD DOES NOT GAIN ON THE MARK.

If the wind is from the northeast, a boat on starboard tack can sail a course which is closer to the weather mark. Therefore, he is sailing closer to the objective (the windward mark) than a boat on port tack, who may not be able to gain any distance on the mark (Figure 33). If the wind shifts to the northwest and the starboard tack boat continues you will find him either not gaining on the mark or sailing away from it (Figure 34). The boat on port tack would have the course which is much more direct. Ideally, you would want to sail on the starboard tack when the wind is from the northeast, and port tack when the wind is from the northwest. By doing this you take advantage of the shifting wind, sail a much shorter distance to the weather mark, and are much closer to the mean wind (Figure 35). The question is, "How do I go about doing this?"

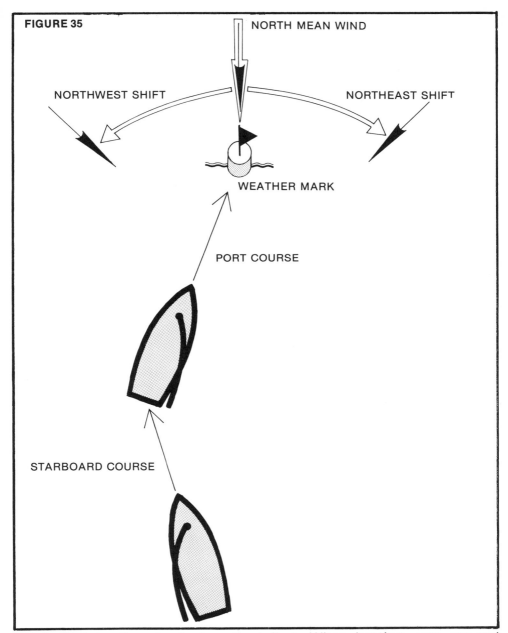

FIGURE 35

NORTH MEAN WIND

NORTHWEST SHIFT

NORTHEAST SHIFT

WEATHER MARK

PORT COURSE

STARBOARD COURSE

Let's take the simplest method first. When beating, you are not steering a straight line. As we said before, you set the boat up to produce the maximum power you can use efficiently, but after that you constantly try to steer into the wind to keep your boat at its most efficient angle to the wind. The technique is very easy. Slowly round into the wind by letting the

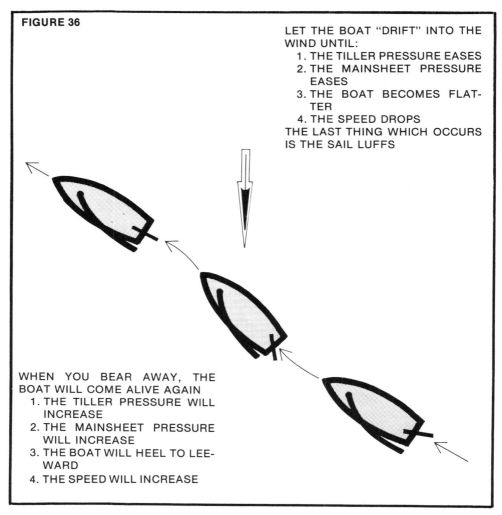

FIGURE 36

LET THE BOAT "DRIFT" INTO THE WIND UNTIL:
1. THE TILLER PRESSURE EASES
2. THE MAINSHEET PRESSURE EASES
3. THE BOAT BECOMES FLATTER
4. THE SPEED DROPS
THE LAST THING WHICH OCCURS IS THE SAIL LUFFS

WHEN YOU BEAR AWAY, THE BOAT WILL COME ALIVE AGAIN
1. THE TILLER PRESSURE WILL INCREASE
2. THE MAINSHEET PRESSURE WILL INCREASE
3. THE BOAT WILL HEEL TO LEEWARD
4. THE SPEED WILL INCREASE

boat drift into the wind. As you approach the source of the wind, the sail will begin to luff. Most people will look for this luff before steering away. However, a luffing sail is a final indicator that they are sailing too close to the wind. It is much better to round slowly into the wind and **feel the boat**. As you get to the point where the sail will luff, several things happen. Boat speed will fall off and the boat will become flatter in the water. There will be less tiller pressure, the mainsheet traveler pressure will diminish, the boat will begin to feel as if it is slowing down and, finally, the sail will luff (Figure 36). Ideally, you steer away from the wind to regain your boat speed just before the sail luffs. The moment you bear away you will feel the boat come alive again as it moves out from underneath you. Then it is a simple matter of once more starting a rounding motion slowly into the wind.

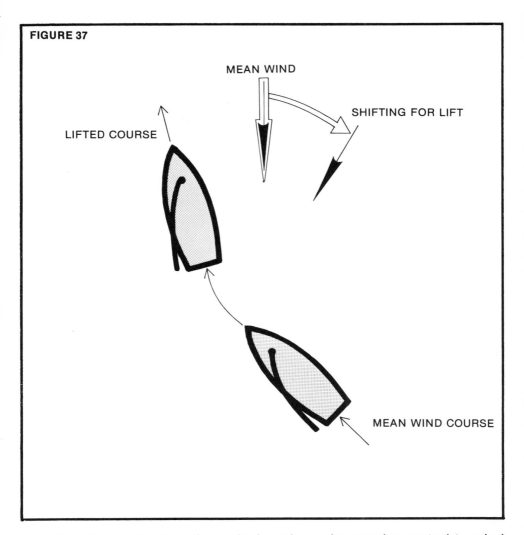

FIGURE 37

MEAN WIND

SHIFTING FOR LIFT

LIFTED COURSE

MEAN WIND COURSE

This time pull either the mainsheet in or the traveler control to windward. This keeps the sail driving a little bit longer. As the boat performance drops off, ease the mainsheet or traveler and drive away from the wind to regain speed. These techniques keep you as close to the wind as possible and, in turn, permit you to spot wind shifts much sooner. If you are on starboard tack and the wind shifts to the northeast, you will be able to steer closer and closer into the wind. You have detected what is known as a **lift** (Figure 37). You will know when the wind shifts either to north or northwest as the sail will luff immediately, automatically completing half of your roll tack. This is called a **header**. If you complete the roll tack, your new tack is a lifted course (Figure 38).

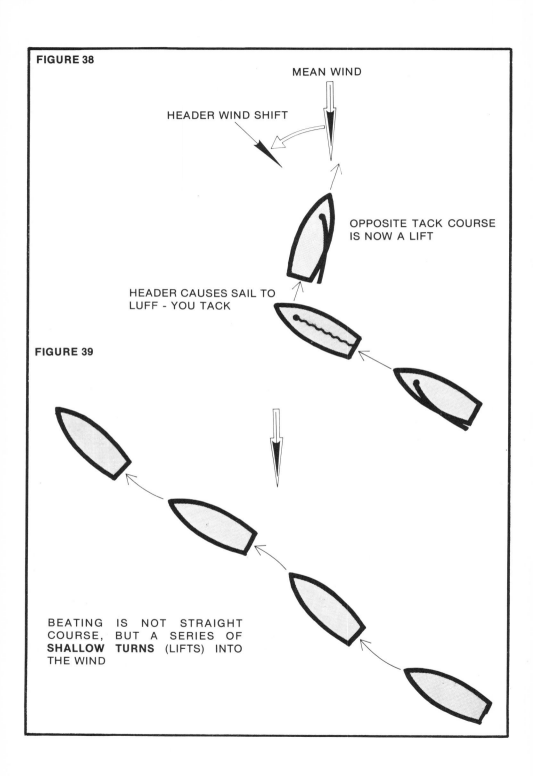

FIGURE 38

MEAN WIND

HEADER WIND SHIFT

OPPOSITE TACK COURSE IS NOW A LIFT

HEADER CAUSES SAIL TO LUFF - YOU TACK

FIGURE 39

BEATING IS NOT STRAIGHT COURSE, BUT A SERIES OF **SHALLOW TURNS** (LIFTS) INTO THE WIND

SELECTING AND EXECUTING THE PROPER START GIVES ONE A GREAT ADVANTAGE AT THE START OF A RACE.

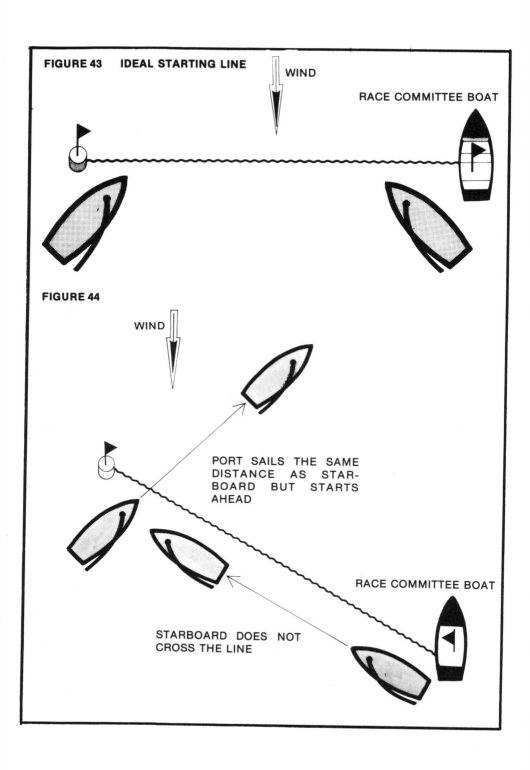

FIGURE 43   IDEAL STARTING LINE

WIND

RACE COMMITTEE BOAT

FIGURE 44

WIND

PORT SAILS THE SAME DISTANCE AS STAR-BOARD BUT STARTS AHEAD

RACE COMMITTEE BOAT

STARBOARD DOES NOT CROSS THE LINE

12 THE STARTING LINE

Most race committees try to set up a starting line that is perpendicular to the mean wind, thereby making both port and starboard tacks equal on the line. They hope that when the start comes the fleet will spread out down the line, with the absence of bunching at either end. Setting a balanced line is a difficult task, as most race committee chairmen will readily admit (Figure 43). In actual practice, most starting lines do not balance equally, and have an end that favors one tack or the other. By a **favored tack** I mean that the line is arranged in such a way that on one tack you can sail across the line at a steeper angle, headed more directly toward the weather mark. Since it takes you less time to sail through a starting line on that tack, and since the favored end is further to windward, it is important to choose correctly. Let's take an extreme example to illustrate what is happening at the favored end of the line.

Set a starting line at 45 degrees to the wind so it more or less approximates the starboard tack. The committee boat is on the starboard end of the line and the bouy end to port. We will use two boats, one at the committee boat end and one at the bouy end, and put them on opposite tacks. At the start, the starboard tack is on the line right at the committee boat, while the port tack boat is moving at the bouy end of the line. You can see that as the starboard tack boat sails down the line he is not gaining on it, but rather his course is parallel to it. When the starboard tack boat comes even with the bouy end of the line, he has not crossed the line, while at the same time the port tack boat has sailed that same distance to windward, and thereby established an early lead. The favored end of the line is the one closer to the wind (Figure 44). If you were to start at the unfavored end, you start the length of the starting line behind. Now the difficult question is, "How do we determine which end of the line is favored?"

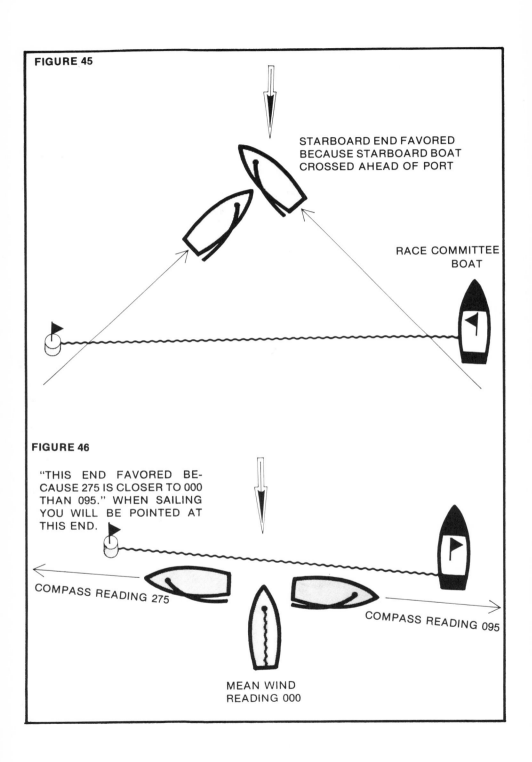

FIGURE 45

STARBOARD END FAVORED
BECAUSE STARBOARD BOAT
CROSSED AHEAD OF PORT

RACE COMMITTEE
BOAT

FIGURE 46

"THIS END FAVORED BE-
CAUSE 275 IS CLOSER TO 000
THAN 095." WHEN SAILING
YOU WILL BE POINTED AT
THIS END.

COMPASS READING 275

COMPASS READING 095

MEAN WIND
READING 000

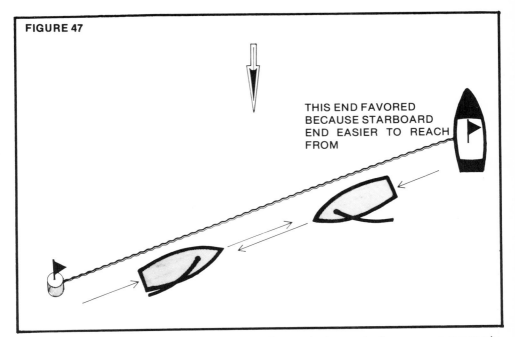

FIGURE 47

THIS END FAVORED
BECAUSE STARBOARD
END EASIER TO REACH
FROM

Race committees rarely set up such an obvious choice as our example. However, there are several methods to determine which end is favored. Perhaps the easiest one is to have a trusted friend sail with you. Before the race, start at one end of the line while your friend starts at the opposite end on opposite tacks. As you sail and converge, whoever passes in front of the other has started at the favored end of the line on the favored tack (Figure 45). It is important that you start at approximately the same time and that both of you sail your boats as fast as possible, so as not to get a false reading. It is also helpful to swap ends of the line so that you balance out any sailing ability.

The second method is by use of the compass. Point the boat directly into the wind, noting on the compass the source of the wind. Then simply reach down the line on one tack and then the other, both times noting your compass course. You will find that the course which is closest to the wind bearing will point you at the favored end of the line (Figure 46).

A third method is somewhat cruder than the other two. Find the tack which is easiest to reach on by sailing up and down the line. Determine on which tack you are furthest away from the wind. The indicators are: the distance the sail is over the side of the boat, how long it takes you to sail the line, and your angle to the line. The tack which is closest to running is the favored tack, and hence the favored end of the line will be behind you (Figure 47). This method is not as accurate as the others, but it will help you determine the favored end of the line.

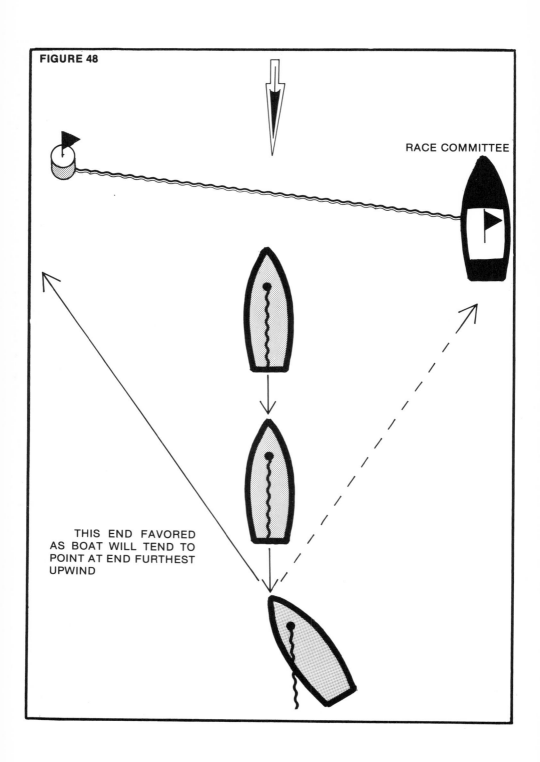

FIGURE 48

RACE COMMITTEE

THIS END FAVORED
AS BOAT WILL TEND TO
POINT AT END FURTHEST
UPWIND

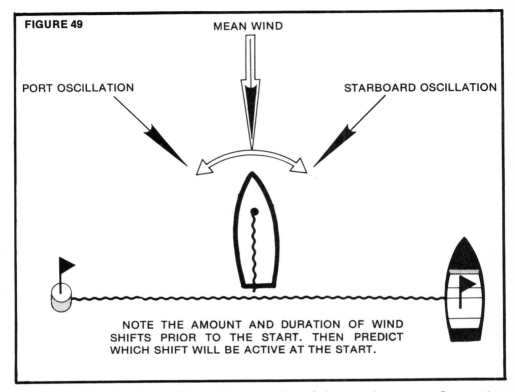

FIGURE 49

MEAN WIND

PORT OSCILLATION

STARBOARD OSCILLATION

NOTE THE AMOUNT AND DURATION OF WIND SHIFTS PRIOR TO THE START. THEN PREDICT WHICH SHIFT WILL BE ACTIVE AT THE START.

A fourth method is almost the opposite of the previous one. Get to the middle of the line and sail head to the wind. As you remain head to the wind and begin to drift backwards, the bow of the boat will point towards the favored end of the line, as it will be the end furthest upwind (Figure 48).

As you can see, there are a number of methods for determining the favored end of the line. However, there are some other things that should effect your choice. First, you must note the windshifts. If the wind is oscillating through a wide arc and the starting line is set to the mean wind, the favored end of the line will depend on which oscillation is active during the start. This is why it is important to start timing wind shifts as early as possible before the start. By doing so, you will know the duration and direction of any given windshift and can predict with some degree of accuracy the favored end of the line for the start (Figure 49). The second consideration is tide (if you're sailing in an area that is subject to tide). The variance in tide and its effect on the starting line are numerous. The best way to determine the favored end of the line in tidal conditions is the first method we discussed (using a boat at each end of the line sailing toward each other). Wind shifts will play a role, but using this technique will help you balance out the effects of wind, water and tide so that you can accurately determine the favored end.

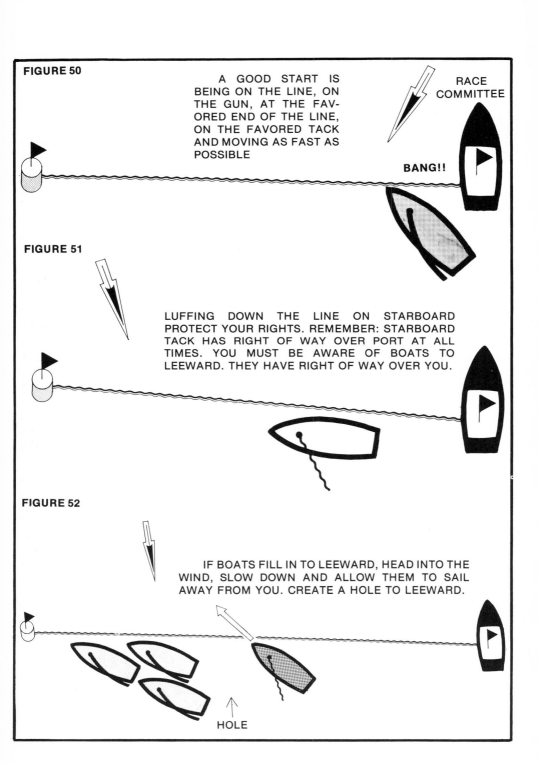

FIGURE 50

A GOOD START IS BEING ON THE LINE, ON THE GUN, AT THE FAVORED END OF THE LINE, ON THE FAVORED TACK AND MOVING AS FAST AS POSSIBLE

RACE COMMITTEE

BANG!!

FIGURE 51

LUFFING DOWN THE LINE ON STARBOARD PROTECT YOUR RIGHTS. REMEMBER: STARBOARD TACK HAS RIGHT OF WAY OVER PORT AT ALL TIMES. YOU MUST BE AWARE OF BOATS TO LEEWARD. THEY HAVE RIGHT OF WAY OVER YOU.

FIGURE 52

IF BOATS FILL IN TO LEEWARD, HEAD INTO THE WIND, SLOW DOWN AND ALLOW THEM TO SAIL AWAY FROM YOU. CREATE A HOLE TO LEEWARD.

HOLE

Now that you have determined the favored end of the starting line, what good is it? The answer is simple. When starting, you want to be at the favored end of the line, on the favored tack, going full speed at the starting signal (Figure 50). This is quite easy to do when there are only one or two boats, but in large fleets a number of good sailors all have the same idea in mind. The favored end of the line will become quite crowded. Getting a good start calls for being **aggressive**, having a **game plan** in mind, and carrying it through **no matter what**.

Most people have trouble starting because they fail to hold to their game plan. They get into a starting situation and, rather than carrying it through, they bail out and become easy prey for an aggressive starter. Coolness under fire and aggressiveness are mandatory for a successful start. Let's set up a game plan and see what happens.

We have already determined that the bouy end of the line is favored and have decided we will negotiate our way to the bouy on starboard tack to preserve our right of way. One method to accomplish this is to coast down the line on starboard tack, with your sails almost luffing, about a minute before the gun (Figure 51). This will allow you to speed up or slow down as you attempt to find a hole and carve out a space in the line of starting boats. What you are trying to protect is an open area on the line for your boat. This area should be clear of other boats to provide you with free air so you can rapidly accelerate, draw away from the line and on to the race course. If prior to the start boats fill in to leeward of you, head up and slow down a little. This allows them to sail closer to the mark and gives you a hole to leeward into which you can reach and accelerate (Figure 52). If they do pass to windward, they steal your air and put you further away from the line (Figure 53). Just prior to the start, when boats get very crowded, luffing a boat to windward can open a space for you to leeward. By getting the windward skipper to pay attention to the boats windward of him (holding the fort, so to speak) for a few seconds, you can quickly reach off into the hole, gain speed and accelerate across the line (Figure 54). At the start your boat will be slightly ahead. They will be slightly behind, effecting each other's wind, and sailing slightly slower than you. Luffing boats to windward can also force those boats over the line early, while you have sailed back to the correct side of the line just prior to the start.

If you abandon your game plan you will find yourself one of the boats that has been luffed over the line or sailed by to windward and you will start the race slightly behind those who have been more aggressive.

Another technique is known as a **dip start**. This technique can only be used when the **one minute** or **five minute rule** (rule 51.1C) is not in effect (see glossary). This calls for sailing to windward of the starting line in such position that you can see the starting pattern develop. From above the line you can pick a hole in the bunches of boats on the line, sail to it, dip down below the line just prior to the start, and come across the line at full speed

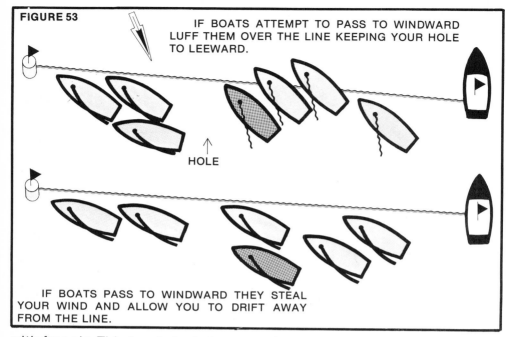

FIGURE 53

IF BOATS ATTEMPT TO PASS TO WINDWARD LUFF THEM OVER THE LINE KEEPING YOUR HOLE TO LEEWARD.

HOLE

IF BOATS PASS TO WINDWARD THEY STEAL YOUR WIND AND ALLOW YOU TO DRIFT AWAY FROM THE LINE.

with free air. This handy technique permits you to determine which oscillation of the wind is in effect for the start because you are to windward of the starting line, uneffected by any of the boats which are racing with you. It allows you to select a hole in the line in which you will not be blanketed or back-winded by other boats (Figure 55). Perhaps the biggest mistake with a dip start is committing yourself to the line too soon and not sailing to the hole closest to the favored end. When you do this, you give the other boats a chance to overtake you either to windward or leeward, hence diminishing the advantage the dip start gives you.

The best advice I can give to anyone trying to determine the best starting line technique is to **practice** starting. Select your game plan or starting technique and stick with it to see how it comes out. It should be fairly obvious a few seconds after the start whether or not your technique worked. Within a dozen starts you should have a comfortable technique which works well for you in your fleet. You will find that by maintaining your game plan your mistakes become easily recognized. If you choose the wrong end of the line, it will become immediately apparent that you are behind, while if you have selected the right end of the line, you will see that you are ahead of those who choose the opposite end. If your on-the-line technique needs modification, you will see boats sailing either over you or out from underneath you. Work on protecting your position on the line. The keys to successful starts are always the same: stick to you game plan and be aggressive.

FIGURE 54

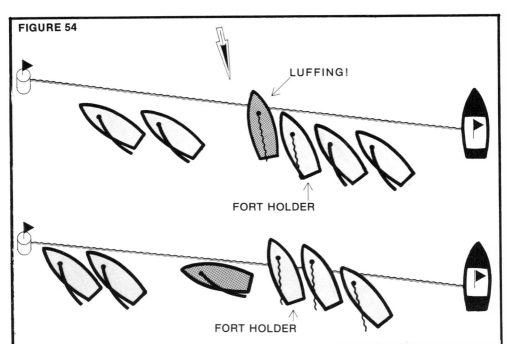

LUFFING!

FORT HOLDER

FORT HOLDER

BY LUFFING JUST PRIOR TO THE START YOU CAN GET THE BOAT IMMEDIATELY TO WINDWARD TO LUFF THE BOATS TO WINDWARD OF HIM AND PREVENT THEM FROM SAILING BY YOU. HE ENDS UP "HOLDING THE FORT" AGAINST THE BOATS TO WEATHER ALLOWING YOU REACH INTO YOUR HOLE TO LEEWARD FOR A GOOD START.

FIGURE 55

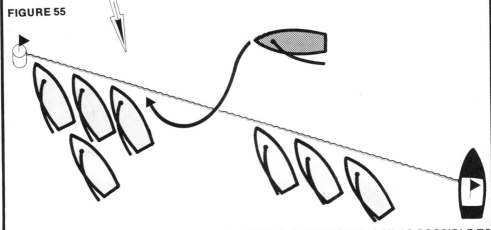

DIP START: SAILING ABOVE THE LINE, SELECTING A HOLE AS CLOSE AS POSSIBLE TO THE FAVORED END AND DIPPING INTO IT JUST PRIOR TO THE START. REMEMBER! YOU HAVE NO RIGHTS OVER THE BOATS TO LEEWARD SO YOU MUST STAY CLEAR OF THEM.

While on the subject of aggression, it is important to remember that a sailboat race does not determine the outcome of the world tomorrow. If in sticking to your game plan you find yourself early, so what? You know now that your starting techniques were attempted too soon. If in your aggressiveness you carried someone over the line with you, you can be sure he will be more careful next time he finds himself next to you on the starting line. Sailboat races only effect the outcome of sailboat races. You can afford to be daring and aggressive. The more you are, the better your start, the better your finish.

The hardest starting technique to master is knowing at all times how close to the line you are. Most people think they are over the line when they are really two to three boat lengths to leeward. The easiest method of finding how close to the line you can sail is by setting a line between the dock and bouy. Have someone stand on the dock and signal you when you cross the line. This type of practice will give you some idea of the visual angles between you and the ends of the starting line (Figure 56).

Another method is to sail to the middle of the line so you are directly between the two ends. Sight over one end to a landmark. When you return to the line and align the landmark, the end of the line and your position, you should be on the line. This technique is difficult with a large fleet because many times other boats sail into your line of sight (Figure 57).

However, with aggressive practice and a well thought out and executed game plan, you will find yourself very close to the line. A good measure of your aggressiveness is whether or not you get recalled at the start. It has been said that a good starter is one who has been recalled twice during a season. The importance of planning your start carefully cannot be over emphasized. If you get a good start and are slightly ahead of the crowd, the air you are sailing in will be stronger than that of the boats behind. With all the fleet converging on the starting line, the air around the line is quite confused. It is not until the fleet has moved away from the starting line and spread out that the wind regains its normal state in the starting area. This can take as long as ten minutes. If you are caught behind at the start you must sail a considerable length of time and distance in confused air, putting you even further behind than if you were to start at the unfavored end of the starting line with clear air. This phenomenon is quite obvious from the race committee boat. The fast sailors will tack for free air, while those who generally finish well down in the fleet will continue on one course, falling steadily behind as they remain in the confused air of other boats.

You can learn about good starting techniques by going to school. By "going to school" I mean, volunteer for race committee duty at least once during the season. Concentrate on where the hot sailors are starting and try to figure out why they did it. Take note of their upwind technique, how they sit in the boat, where the sail is set, where they go on the race course and

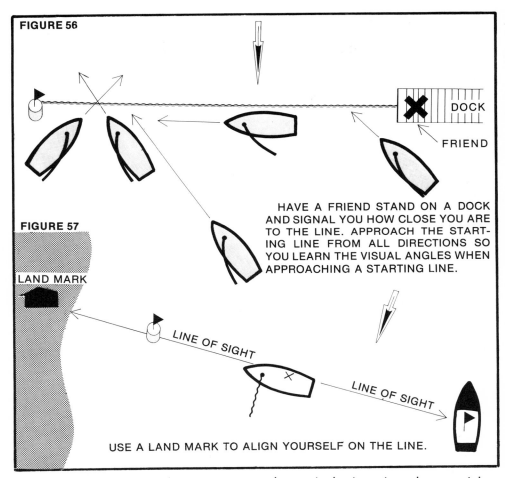

FIGURE 56

DOCK

FRIEND

HAVE A FRIEND STAND ON A DOCK
AND SIGNAL YOU HOW CLOSE YOU ARE
TO THE LINE. APPROACH THE START-
ING LINE FROM ALL DIRECTIONS SO
YOU LEARN THE VISUAL ANGLES WHEN
APPROACHING A STARTING LINE.

FIGURE 57

LAND MARK

LINE OF SIGHT

LINE OF SIGHT

USE A LAND MARK TO ALIGN YOURSELF ON THE LINE.

how they tack. Watch the race as a serious student, not an innocent by-
stander. It is even helpful to take a notepad and jot down their techniques
or adjustments. Remember: in sailing there are so many variables that it's
almost impossible to remember or account for all of them.

In a multiclass regatta, you can "go to school" by watching the starts
prior to your class. Find out where the hot members of each fleet are
starting. Let them help you determine the favored end of the line. If you
know who the fleet champion or fleet leader is, watch his starting
technique and where he goes on the first leg of the course. This ought to
give you a good idea where you should go. By watching the fleets in front,
you can determine the favored side of the course, the wind oscillations and
favored end of the starting line, as well as a number of handy techniques
for your own race. In sailing it is important to learn techniques, skills and
judgements from anyone and anywhere you can.

CHOOSING THE FAVORED END OF THE STARTING LINE CALLS FOR ONE TO CONSIDER WIND SHIFTS, TIDE AND THE FLEET TACTICS. HERE BOTH ENDS SEEM TO BE FAVORED AS A DIFFERENT WIND OSCILLATION IS EFFECTING EITHER END OF THE LINE. MANY TIMES ONE MUST CONSIDER THE WIND CONDITIONS AFTER THE START TO DETERMINE THE FAVORED END OF THE LINE.

13 BEATING AGAIN

Once on the course, it is important to keep your mind on making your boat sail fast and the wind that is effecting you. For the first two minutes of the race, concentrate on making your boat go as fast as possible to carry yourself away from the line and into clean air. If in that time you find yourself in disturbed air, check about you and, if possible, tack away to regain clean air. Once free of the starting line, it is important to keep your mind aimed at the weather mark and alert for windshifts. As mentioned before, the wind does oscillate. If you have taken notes and determined the oscillations before the start, you know you are on the favored tack when starting. It is important to remain on the favored tack for the entire weather leg. This will call for you to roll tack from one tack to the other as the wind oscillates.

Most high-powered skippers will tack when their sail luffs violently. Often they do not plan their roll tack well in advance, but do remain alert to take advantage of the next wind shift. It is a good idea to make note of the compass course for each tack, and to note how far you can steer away from the wind before it is best to be on the opposite tack. You should know whether the wind shift that is effecting you continues to be a lift that brings you closer to the mark, or just a shift to the mean wind, which means you are still gaining on the mark. If the shift is a header, you will know to tack immediately.

Sometimes it is possible to use the shore as your compass. By sighting the shore and noting a position as you sail, you will know if you are gaining on the shore (a lift steering you to windward) or losing on the shore (a header steering you away from the wind). In this way you will always know what kind of gusts you are sailing in without constantly looking at the compass, and you will know if you should tack or not when the next gust reaches you. With very little practice you will discover that your dependency on compass bearings for a short course will diminish. You will have a mental picture of the race course and begin to determine automatically the most efficient course to the weather mark.

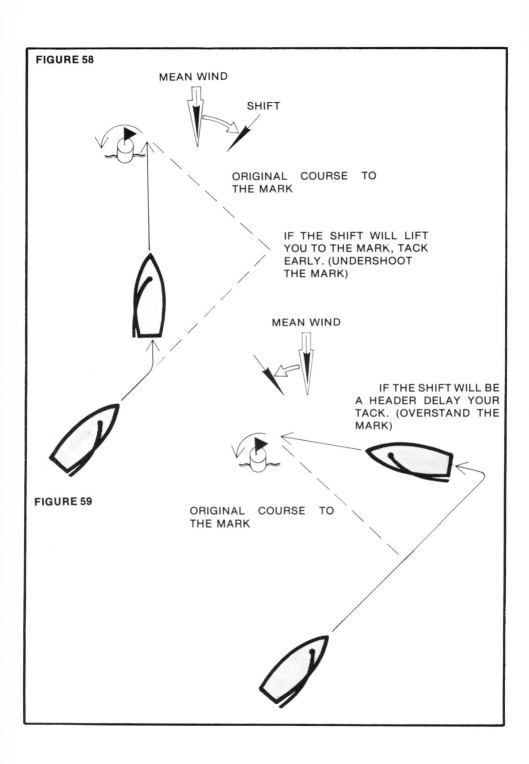

FIGURE 58

MEAN WIND

SHIFT

ORIGINAL COURSE TO THE MARK

IF THE SHIFT WILL LIFT YOU TO THE MARK, TACK EARLY. (UNDERSHOOT THE MARK)

MEAN WIND

IF THE SHIFT WILL BE A HEADER DELAY YOUR TACK. (OVERSTAND THE MARK)

FIGURE 59

ORIGINAL COURSE TO THE MARK

14 BEAT TO REACH

If you have noted the duration of each oscillation and its direction, you will be able to predict the most efficient tack to the weather mark. You will know if you can tack early and expect the wind to shift into a lifting condition, carrying you to the weather mark (Figure 58), or whether you must tack later in anticipation of a header (Figure 59). This information is very useful when approaching the mark and can save valuable time and distance, helping you get around the weather mark ahead of your competitors.

As you approach the weather mark, make as many adjustments as you can before the reach. Set the boom vang, perhaps ease the outhaul, and sometimes start raising the board. As you round the mark, especially in a crowd, the most important thing is to sail fast and get your boat to accelerate onto a plane. This will carry you away from the other boats very quickly. The reason is quite simple. Most people think they must have the spinnaker up and the boat properly trimmed and ready to go as quickly as possible after rounding the mark. However, you can gain quite a bit of time and distance if you simply concentrate on sailing. While the competition is trying to get everything set for the reach, they have to dodge each other, and more than likely will get entangled with themselves. If you pay attention to your steering and reaching techniques, you can plane by them, get safely in front and then make your final adjustments, from spinnaker setting to board raising, much more efficiently.

We discussed earlier the techniques of making a boat go faster on a reach -- constantly trying to nurse the boat onto a plane, moving your weight fore and aft and in and out. We also mentioned steering up in the lulls and driving off in the gusts. Remember these techniques as we continue.

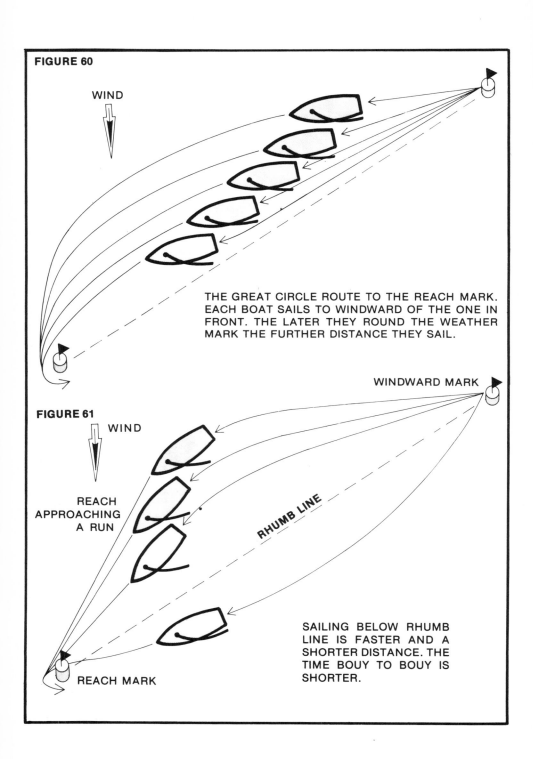

FIGURE 60

WIND

THE GREAT CIRCLE ROUTE TO THE REACH MARK. EACH BOAT SAILS TO WINDWARD OF THE ONE IN FRONT. THE LATER THEY ROUND THE WEATHER MARK THE FURTHER DISTANCE THEY SAIL.

WINDWARD MARK

FIGURE 61

WIND

REACH APPROACHING A RUN

RHUMB LINE

SAILING BELOW RHUMB LINE IS FASTER AND A SHORTER DISTANCE. THE TIME BOUY TO BOUY IS SHORTER.

REACH MARK

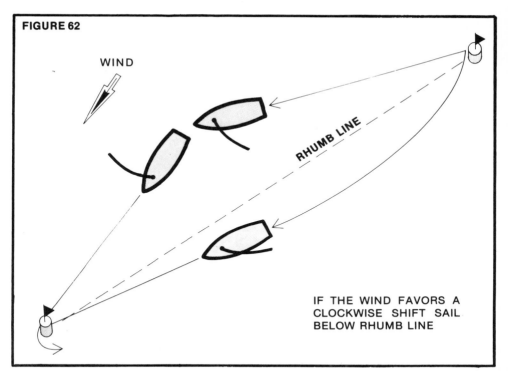

FIGURE 62

WIND

RHUMB LINE

IF THE WIND FAVORS A CLOCKWISE SHIFT SAIL BELOW RHUMB LINE

When you are behind it is important to remember that most people steer their boat to windward on a reach. The fleet or the pack tends to sail windward of the straight line reach because each boat trys to keep its wind free by steering to windward of the boat in front of it. This establishes the "great circle route" to the reach mark, as each successive boat sails a greater distance (Figure 60). As a result, the last quarter to half of the reach leg often turns into a run. An easy technique for passing boats on a reach is to sail to leeward of the **rhumb line** (the straight line course from bouy to bouy). This must be decided at the weather mark. As you approach the reach mark you will be close reaching, sailing faster and traveling a shorter distance than the boats which have sailed high (Figure 61). I have seen sailors pick up a number of boats by using this technique. Not only do they sail a shorter course, but when they arrive at the reach mark, they are the inside boat and have rights to round the bouy. This is a good technique to use when you are behind.

Another technique concerns the oscillation of the wind. If the oscil-lations favor the starboard tack (that is, clockwise in nature), it is generally best to sail low of the rhumb line (Figure 62). If you were to sail high, many times you will get into a position where you are running to the reach mark. If the oscillations are extreme, you may have to jibe to return to the reach mark. This costs you valuable time and distance because you have sailed

considerably out of your way. On the other hand, if the oscillations favor the port tack (that is, counter-clockwise), it is generally best to sail a little high of the rhumb line. If you were to hold low of the rhumb line, you may have to beat to the reach mark.

These rhumb line tendencies depend on two conditions: first, the placement of the reach mark; second, the direction the wind shifts favor. Most race committees set the reach mark to complete an equilateral triangle. For the sake of discussion let's discuss some general rules, assuming this is true.

When you are beating and you discover the wind shifts favor a starboard tack and the first reach is starboard, sail low of the rhumb line. If the shifts favor port and the first reach is starboard, sail above the rhumb line. More simply, when the favored tack and the first reach are the same, sail low; otherwise sail high. Once you round the reach mark, the opposite tendencies are generally true.

Remember that this "rule of rhumb" is a tendency for the entire reach leg. If you over adjust, you could negate the advantages because you begin to sail a greater distance. But if you do not make a firm commitment, you will find yourself sailing with the pack rather than seeking your own fast and efficient route.

Remember, these commitments are made at the beginning of the leg. When rounding the weather mark, you will find it advantageous to immediately commit yourself above or below the rhumb line. This will quickly clear you from other boats and allow you to press the advantage gained that much longer.

15 REACH TO BEAT

As you complete the first triangle of an olympic course, there are several things of which you should be aware. First, the fleet has spread out so mark roundings are somewhat more orderly. This means you can make your mark roundings more intelligently, as you need not be as concerned with other boats clustered around the mark about to be rounded. You can concentrate on the proper method of rounding the mark. Most people steer straight at a mark and then try to steer their boat sharply around it. They initiate their turn slightly before the mark and when they round, they slide by it (Figure 63). A clever sailor is ever mindful of this and will take advantage of another sailor who puts himself in this predicament. A clever sailor starts this turn further away from the mark so that when the boat is finished turning, its rounding motion is very close to the departure side of the mark (Figure 64).

The next thing a clever sailor does is avoid getting caught on the outside of a rounding maneuver (Figure 65). He never allows several boats to sail between him and the mark. If he finds himself approaching a mark in this position, he will delay his rounding. Even though he rounds behind those boats, he is to weather of them and able to tack much sooner than if he had maintained his course and rounded outside (Figure 66). This technique works extremely well in large fleets, and in light wind conditions, when the fleet often gets bunched at the leeward mark. The boats which rounded the weather mark behind the leaders drift on top of those boats that rounded in front, and by the time everyone reaches the leeward mark, they are strung out across the race course. The poor fellow on the outside of this mess can lose many, many places. But by simply slowing down and sailing behind all these boats, one can consolidate his loses and round the mark in far better shape. Rounding the mark on the outside of a number of boats

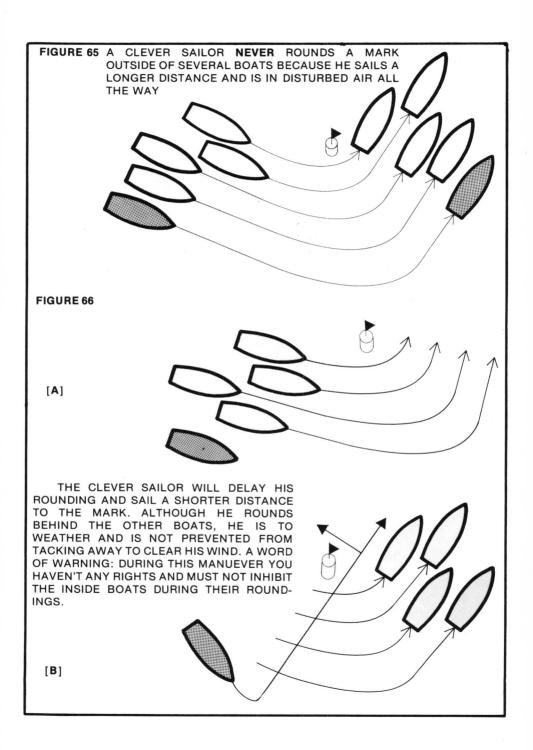

FIGURE 65 A CLEVER SAILOR **NEVER** ROUNDS A MARK OUTSIDE OF SEVERAL BOATS BECAUSE HE SAILS A LONGER DISTANCE AND IS IN DISTURBED AIR ALL THE WAY

FIGURE 66

[A]

THE CLEVER SAILOR WILL DELAY HIS ROUNDING AND SAIL A SHORTER DISTANCE TO THE MARK. ALTHOUGH HE ROUNDS BEHIND THE OTHER BOATS, HE IS TO WEATHER AND IS NOT PREVENTED FROM TACKING AWAY TO CLEAR HIS WIND. A WORD OF WARNING: DURING THIS MANUEVER YOU HAVEN'T ANY RIGHTS AND MUST NOT INHIBIT THE INSIDE BOATS DURING THEIR ROUND-INGS.

[B]

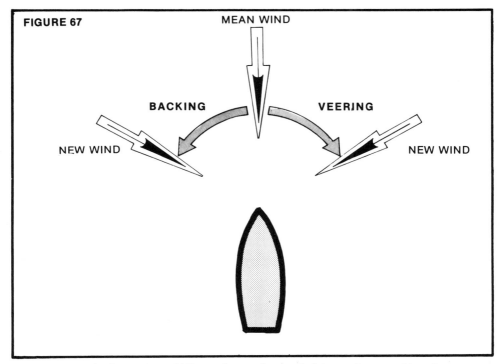

FIGURE 67

MEAN WIND

BACKING   VEERING

NEW WIND   NEW WIND

puts you at their mercy. Although you have rights as leeward boat, you cannot tack to take advantage of the next windshift until they do. However, most of the time the inside boats have a shorter distance to sail and therefore sail by the outside boat, giving him bad air. If you are caught in this predicament, you must tack away to free your air as quickly as possible. You will be starting the next leg of the course far behind those boats which rounded to the inside of you.

It is also important to remember windshifts. We have already discussed the mean wind and the wind shifts to either side of it -- what we call an osolation. However, another thing occurs to confuse the issue. The wind either **backs** or **veers**. This means that the entire mean wind system shifts either clockwise or counter-clockwise. A clockwise movement is called **veering**, and a counter-clockwise movement is called **backing** (Figure 67). A veering wind will favor a starboard tack and the starboard side of the course. A backing wind will favor a port tack and the port side of the course.

The time it takes you to complete the first triangle of an olympic course is ample time for the veering or backing effect to take place. If you were diligent about taking notes of earlier wind patterns, you will readily know if the wind has veered or backed as you depart the leeward mark because the tacking maximums and minimums of your compass bearings

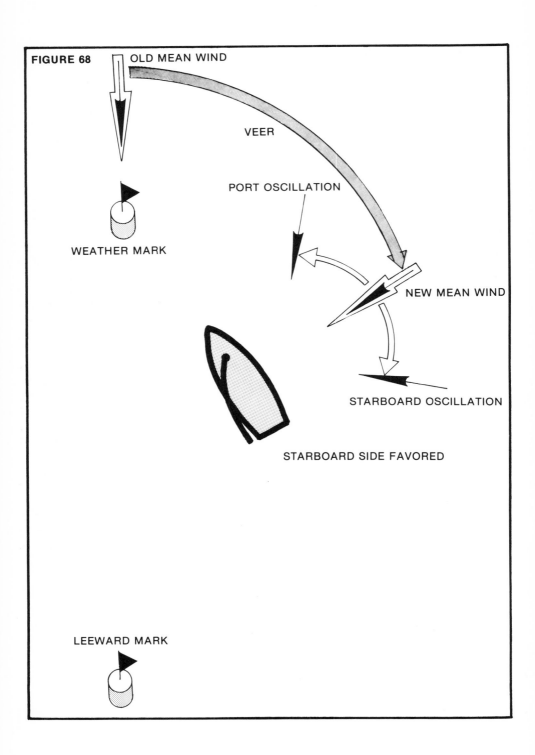

FIGURE 68

OLD MEAN WIND

VEER

PORT OSCILLATION

WEATHER MARK

NEW MEAN WIND

STARBOARD OSCILLATION

STARBOARD SIDE FAVORED

LEEWARD MARK

will have changed slightly. If you have found that starboard tack is even more favored, you can safely say that the wind has veered slightly. However, if you find that the port tack is slightly favored, you can predict a backing wind. This is quite helpful in choosing the side of the course which you should sail for the next leg. If the wind is veering, you should favor the starboard side. The reason is quite simple. A veering wind will move clockwise and therefore lift you on starboard tack. The oscillations about the mean wind will have all moved clockwise. (Figure 68). The same applies for backing wind, only in a counter-clockwise direction'. A word of warning, though: don't be fooled by radically oscillating winds. If in your wind analysis prior to the start you find large shifts in wind direction, then it is probably wise to play the middle of the course and take advantage of the shifts as they favor both port and starboard tacks.

To round out our discussion of windshifts, I would like to call attention to a phenomena I will call a **rounding veer** (it can also be a **rounding back**, but for an example we will use a rounding veer). This occurs when the wind, for some reason, be it a passing thunderstorm or front, causes a continuous and radical change of wind direction. Some people call this a **round house lift**. It generally penalizes those sailors out in front because they have been taking advantage of the wind effecting them and have not predicted this radical change in wind direction. If you find yourself in this situation, the best thing you can do is sail toward it. That is, try to get to the inside of the shift. The longer you wait, the further you will have to sail. This is especially true if you have just rounded the mark. You will find that if you remain on the lifted tack from the mark to your destination, you will sail a great circle route rather than a direct one. However, if you were to immediately tack and sail into the lift for a short distance and then return to the lifted tack, your course will be more direct to your objective.

On the second beat of an olympic course you are in a position to take advantage of every windshift. You no longer have to worry about other boats effecting your course and your desire to take advantage of windshifts. If you are behind, it is important to go to school again, this is, watch the leaders. Find out which side of the course they favor. Are they favoring that side because the wind is veering or backing? By watching them you will know what kind of wind will be effecting you, enabling you to put your boat in a position to take advantage of the shifting wind.

You will find that you will be gaining not only on those boats around you, but will be closing the gap on the leaders. Once you are with the leaders, display your superior knowledge of how to make your boat sail fast.

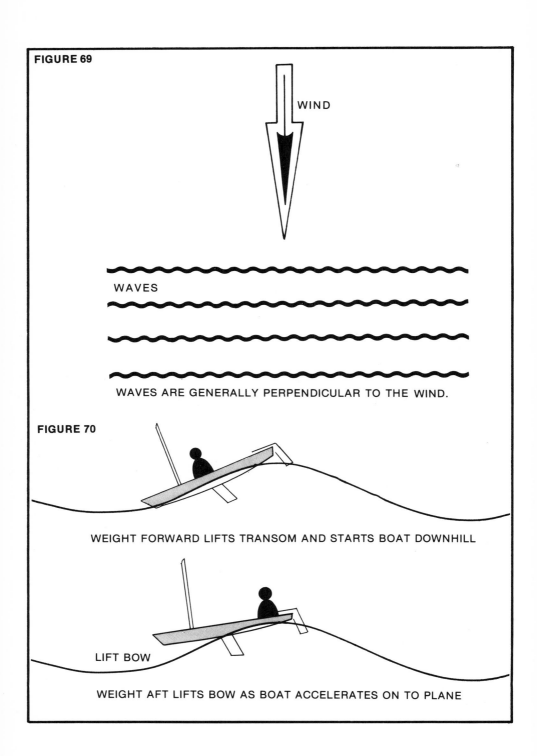

FIGURE 69

WIND

WAVES

WAVES ARE GENERALLY PERPENDICULAR TO THE WIND.

FIGURE 70

WEIGHT FORWARD LIFTS TRANSOM AND STARTS BOAT DOWNHILL

LIFT BOW

WEIGHT AFT LIFTS BOW AS BOAT ACCELERATES ON TO PLANE

16 BEAT TO RUN

By the time you get to the weather mark for the second time, the fleet will be spread out even more. The boats will be widely spaced and bunching at the weather mark will be at a minimum. Again, it is important to note what wind shift will be in effect as you approach the weather mark. Remember, if you can sail to the mark on a lift, you can tack earlier than if you have to sail to the mark on a header. If you remember this, you won't find yourself reaching to return to the mark or ending up short and having to make two quick tacks to round the mark properly.

Rounding the weather mark for the run is the time to display your fast crew work. With the absence of boats, your prime objective is to get your boat set up for down wind sailing as quickly as possible. Set the spinnaker, pole out the jib, pull up the board, make your sail adjustments, and then concentrate on making the boat go as fast as possible down wind.

Most of us have heard the term **surfing**. In sailing, surfing means getting your boat pointed down the face of a wave to take advantage of not only the speed of the wave but the energy it carries. In general, waves line themselves perpendicular to the direction of the mean wind (Figure 69). Thus, when running you are going with them. Water weighs approximately 64 lbs. per cubic foot. Therefore, even a small wave will effect your boat. It is important not to fight waves, but rather to use them to propel you forward. Five cubic feet of water is equal to 320 lbs., as much as most small one design sailboats weigh. Putting your small one design against a large wave is a losing battle. It is better to use the wave and let it push the boat.

As you sail downwind and point the boat down a wave, you will feel the boat accelerate slightly because the transom becomes higher than the bow and your boat is actually pointed downhill (Figure 70). As the boat

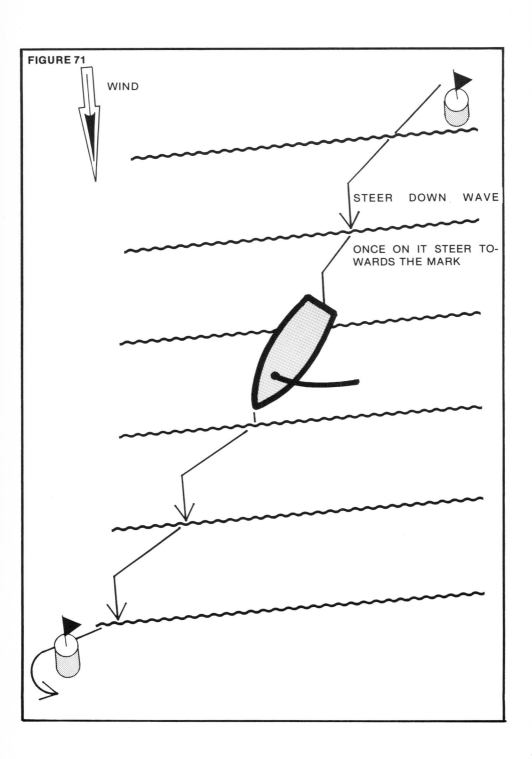

FIGURE 71

WIND

STEER DOWN WAVE

ONCE ON IT STEER TO-
WARDS THE MARK

accelerates, the apparent wind will move forward. By bearing away slightly and pulling in the sail, you will sustain the time and distance that you remain on that wave. The longer you are on that wave, the faster you will be able to sail the downwind leg of the course.

The same techniques of nursing your boat onto a plane are applied when surfing. By moving forward as the wave comes behind, you will help push the bow down and start the boat on its downhill slide. As the boat accelerates down the wave, move back to lift the bow and get the boat to plane. At the same time, sheet in as the apparent wind moves forward. With practice, you will begin to sustain your time on a given wave.

But mastering surfing isn't enough. It is important to sail faster than the waves because they are moving slower than the wind. To accomplish this, take note of the wave patterns. Sail your boat down the waves where they are the largest, gain speed, and then blast over the next wave where it is the smallest. This will call for you to sail sometimes by the lee and sometimes slightly to windward because you are angling yourself on and over the waves.

The same techniques are used to promote surfing while on a reach. While reaching, however, you are constantly sailing at an angle to the waves. Because the waves are moving to leeward, remember you can be carried to leeward of the reach mark. To promote surfing while reaching requires you to select a wave and steer with it, sometimes approaching a run (Figure 71). As the wave picks you up and the boat begins to accelerate, start steering to windward and sheeting in. The boat will accelerate further as you begin to multiply your boat's acceleration, the wave speed and the apparent wind. Once you drop off the wave, sheet out immediately because the apparent wind will quickly move aft and the oversheeted sail will spin your boat about the board. By using these techniques to promote planing and surfing, you will find your reaching legs are much faster.

One question that might be in your mind is, "How big a wave do you need to surf?" Because water weighs so much, it doesn't take much of a wave to develop considerable force. I suggest trying to surf every wave, using every wave to its best advantage. You will find yourself concentrating on making the boat go fast and letting the actual surfing become second nature.

Keep your mind alert to windshifts. Just because you are sailing downwind doesn't mean that the wind remains in one direction. It continually shifts back and forth and each gust will arrive at your boat from a new direction. It is important to take advantage of all these shifts. One of the best ways is to keep the wind at right angles to the sail. To do this, it's helpful to tie a telltail to the middle of the boom. If you sail your boat and make mainsheet adjustments in such a way that the telltail stays at right angles to the sail, you can be assured that you are going directly downward (Figure 72). The old rule of the shortest distance between two points is a

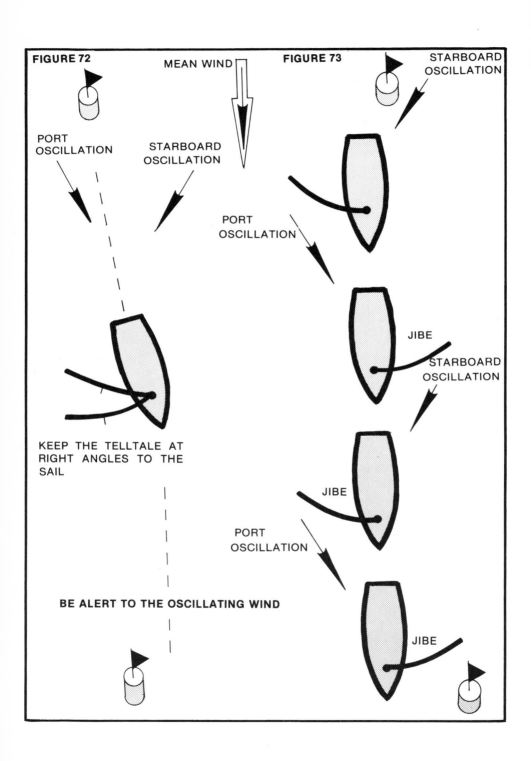

FIGURE 72

MEAN WIND

FIGURE 73

STARBOARD OSCILLATION

PORT OSCILLATION

STARBOARD OSCILLATION

PORT OSCILLATION

JIBE

STARBOARD OSCILLATION

KEEP THE TELLTALE AT RIGHT ANGLES TO THE SAIL

JIBE

PORT OSCILLATION

BE ALERT TO THE OSCILLATING WIND

JIBE

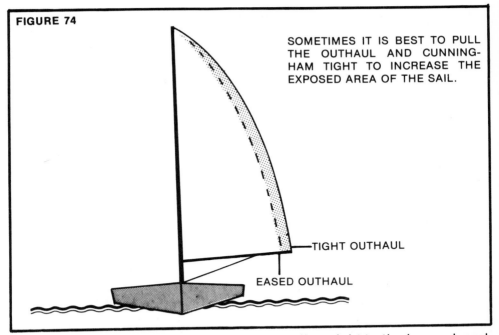

FIGURE 74

SOMETIMES IT IS BEST TO PULL THE OUTHAUL AND CUNNING-HAM TIGHT TO INCREASE THE EXPOSED AREA OF THE SAIL.

TIGHT OUTHAUL

EASED OUTHAUL

straight line applies downward. If you can sail straight to the leeward mark, you will generally get there faster than someone who sails off to one side. However, several factors can effect this decision. First, if you can sail at a considerably higher rate of speed by surfing at an angle to the waves, it might pay to sail some extra distance. Another factor is the oscillating wind. In oscillating shifts when you attempt to sail straight downwind at all times, you will find yourself steering as erratic course in your attempts to keep the wind at right angles to the sail. In these conditions it is better to sail straight to the mark and jibe when necessary to take advantage of each shift (Figure 73). Remember the rules we discussed earlier for making your boat go fast on a run.

We mentioned before that easing the outhaul and the cunningham pro-duces a large pocket shape in the sail. Sometimes, however, it is best to pull the sail tight with the cunningham and/or outhaul, thereby increasing the exposed area of the sail. This can be extremely helpful in light air where it is difficult to keep a full sail drawing. Each wave and movement of the boat seems to shake the sail enough to cause it to collapse (Figure 74). The same adjustment can also be helpful in heavier air, as you will find the sail will lose its tendency to twist, deform and become hard to control. As you approach the leeward mark to begin the final leg of the olympic course, get the boat set up early. In other words, adjust the sail, the board and your position so that you are ready to sail the weather leg before rounding the leeward mark.

SOME SKIPPERS WILL DO ANYTHING TO GET ACROSS THE FINISH LINE.

17 THE LAST BEAT

The last beat is the most important -- it determines your finishing position. It is still possible to go from last place to first place (as long as the first boat hasn't already finished) and it is also possible to go from first place to last place. Concentration becomes critical. The longer the race course, the stronger the wind and the more races in a given day, the more fatigued you will become. Physical fatigue is one of your biggest enemies in high performance racing. A person who is physically fatigued is not mentally alert. His mind is filled with thoughts of aching muscles and sore hands, not windshifts, wave patterns, weight placement, sail adjustment and strategy. It has been said that for every minute you fail to concentrate while racing you lose from three to ten minutes of sustained boat speed. And you never regain the loss of time and distance. I am sure there are people who will argue this point, but unless you are giving one hundred per cent you are bound to make mistakes.

What does it take to be in good physical condition? Sailing isn't a brutal sport like football, yet it requires tremendous physical energy, and while sailing isn't a sedate sport like chess, it requires the same amount of mental durability with regard to tactics and strategy. Sailing is a combination of "the best of these two worlds", requiring good physical conditioning and sound mental discipline.

Most fast sailors have a very loose program for physical conditioning. They keep their muscles in constant use, and this allows them to be ready to sail at a moment's notice. They condition their minds by analyzing situations and discussing areas of improvement. Push ups, sit ups and jogging are excellent ways of developing your sailing muscles, but they become quite boring after a time. I suggest supplementing these types of exercises with the wall lean (as discussed in the chapter on hiking). This exercise conditions your muscles and your mind to function under extreme distress. You will find the longer you can hold the wall lean position, the longer you will be able to hike out over the side of your boat.

But back to the race course. As you get ready to round the leeward mark and sail the last weather leg to the finish, it is important that you round this mark as quickly and smartly as possible. The techniques we discussed before apply again. However, by this time in the race, most of the boats will be spread out enough that the mark roundings are more of a parade than a chance to gain places. This is why it is important to round the mark, get away from it and headed towards the finish line as quickly and efficiently as possible.

To accomplish this, your mark rounding from a run to a beat must be smooth and orderly. Sail wide of the mark when approaching it so that you can round up tightly as you pass by it. This allows you to trim your sails for the beat in a smooth, efficient manner because your turn is somewhat wider, thus slowing the transition from running to beating. With practice you will find this technique allows you to trim sails for the point of sailing you are passing through, thus making a smooth transition from running to beating. As you pass through a reaching position, you will have the sail set for a reach, and as you approach your beating position, your sail will approach a beating position (Figure 75). In this way you do not overpower the boat, nor do you place it in a position where the boat is pointed in one direction with the sail trimmed for another.

This technique eliminates the situation created by many sailors who habitually round a mark from a run and find their sails flapping as they try to sail away. Their turn was so sharp that it was impossible for them ot trim their sails. I am sure you have seen one of your competitors parked next to the leeward mark, pointed on a beat with his sails flapping madly in the wind (Figure 76).

While beating, there are other areas about which you should be concerned. First, the angle of heel. Excessive heeling causes an increase in **leeway**. (Leeway is the amount the boat slides sideways.) The degree of leeway is different for every boat, but, in general, as a boat heels the amount of leeway increases. This leeway in turn increases weather helm (the tendency of the boat to steer into the wind). As the boat slides sideways, the rudder feels this side slippage. You detect it through the tiller as weather helm and steer against it. With the boat excessively heeled, the rudder blade is no longer vertical and the offset rudder lifts the transom rather than steers it. As the transom lifts out of the water, it begins to slide to leeward, further amplifying weather helm.

Most one design racing sailboats perform best upwind when sailed flat. Sailing flat presents the maximum lateral resistance plane, preventing side slippage and exposing the maximum sail area for drive. However, "flat" is a relative term and will vary from boat to boat. Allowing the boat to heel slightly will reduce the wetted surface, that is, the skin area of the boat

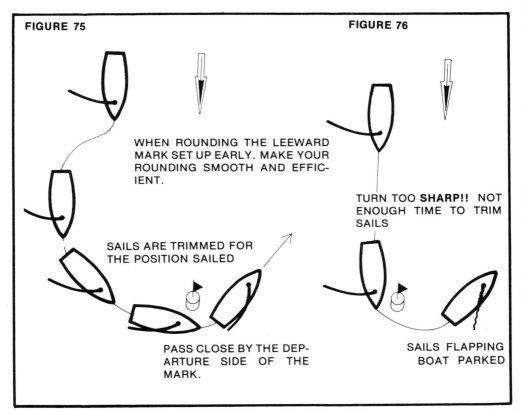

FIGURE 75   **FIGURE 76**

WHEN ROUNDING THE LEEWARD MARK SET UP EARLY. MAKE YOUR ROUNDING SMOOTH AND EFFIC-IENT.

TURN TOO **SHARP!!** NOT ENOUGH TIME TO TRIM SAILS

SAILS ARE TRIMMED FOR THE POSITION SAILED

PASS CLOSE BY THE DEP-ARTURE SIDE OF THE MARK.

SAILS FLAPPING BOAT PARKED

which is immersed in the water. Reducing this area reduces the friction of the water against the hull and permits the boat to be sailed slightly faster. The fast sailor is looking for a balance between reduced wetted surface, leeway and maximum speed.

In light to medium airs, this simple technique is easily maintained by adjusting your weight. However, in heavy gusty conditions it is generally difficult to maintain a precise angle of heel. In these conditions sail the boat as flat as possible to prevent excessive leeway and provide maximum drive.

Another thing to be aware of is waves. As mentioned before, waves are generally traveling with and perpendicular to the mean wind. While beating they are constantly trying to set you to leeward. Most of the time your boat has enough power to overcome the waves and make some headway against them. However, with each wave trying to set you back, it is advantageous to confront them as little as possible. One of the best techniques was discussed earlier, that is, as the wave approaches, steer into it, and once passed, steer away from the wind and drive down the backside. This allows the boat to accelerate as the wind increases and maintain its speed as the wind decreases because as the wave approaches, the boat rises higher and higher on the wave. More and more sail is being exposed to the wind. By steering into the wind you not only maintain balance and drive, but allow the boat to take the wave almost bow on. As the wave crest passes the boat falls lower and lower into the trough between the waves and begins to lose wind. By driving away from the wind you will maintain speed as the wind decreases. This handy technique permits you to sail your boat without fighting the waves.

The rules of finding the weak spots in the waves still apply. If you have an opportunity to sail through a smaller set of waves or broken area in the wave pattern, do so. It will require less energy to drive the boat through those areas than through the larger waves and therefore is faster.

Finishing is the most important part of the race. Everything discussed to this point has been aimed to get you to the finish line first. Many race committees will set a finish line which is not necessarily directly between the leeward and windward mark. Many times it is off to one side. As you are running, you should take note of the position of the finish line and, if possible, note its angle to the wind. This can save you considerable time and distance searching for the finish line when you have rounded the leeward mark. If the finish line is off to one side, you will know it early. By analyzing its position with the wind oscillations in mind, you should be able to predict the quickest route to the finishing line.

The finish line, like the starting line, can have a favored end. The favored end of the finishing line is the one closest to the leeward mark, the one which allows you to finish most quickly and directly. Since it is impossible to test the finish line as you would test the starting line, it is imperative that you analyse it carefully. I have seen many races lost because the lead boat sailed for the wrong end of the line, thus allowing the boat behind to finish first at the favored end.

As you approach the finish line, predict which tack would be favored for the next gust. As in rounding the weather mark, this will allow you to either tack early to the finish line and be lifted to it, or require you to tack later and return to it. You want to cross the finish line at the steepest angle possible at the end which is closest to the leeward mark. Only then can you be assured you have sailed the shortest distance between the leeward mark and the finishing line (Figure 77).

There are two good methods of determining the favored end of the finish line. First, ask a member of the race committee (after the race, ashore) which end and tack was favored. Second "go to school" prior to and after finishing. Note how the leaders and the bulk of the fleet cross the line. Do these observations coincide with your own tactics? This may sound like hindsight, but observing and noting others will make it easier to identify the favored end when you approach in first place with others in hot pursuit. Once you have finished, clear the line as quickly as possible. Sail

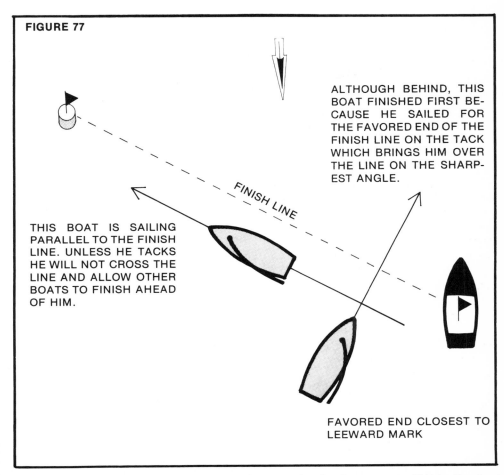

FIGURE 77

ALTHOUGH BEHIND, THIS BOAT FINISHED FIRST BECAUSE HE SAILED FOR THE FAVORED END OF THE FINISH LINE ON THE TACK WHICH BRINGS HIM OVER THE LINE ON THE SHARPEST ANGLE.

FINISH LINE

THIS BOAT IS SAILING PARALLEL TO THE FINISH LINE. UNLESS HE TACKS HE WILL NOT CROSS THE LINE AND ALLOW OTHER BOATS TO FINISH AHEAD OF HIM.

FAVORED END CLOSEST TO LEEWARD MARK

well away from the line to stay out of the path of other racers. If it is the last race of the day, practice all your racing techniques as you sail in. Analyze what has happened on the race course. Try to pass as many boats as you can on the way in. This will give you some idea if your techniques are working. As you sail by someone, ask them if you are trimmed properly. Perhaps their suggestions will help you do better next time.

AUTHOR JACK EVANS AND ARTIST RANDALL DE LEEUW AFTER THE 1975 EASTERN LAKES SPRING FORCE 5 CHAMPIONSHIP AT GREEN POND, N.J. EVANS FINISHED FIRST, DE LEEUW SECOND.

18 THE CLUBHOUSE

This book was put together with the idea that sailors make boats go fast. I have presented a number of ideas on how you can make your boat go faster. Perhaps not all these techniques will work for you, but they are available to you. They only require practice and patience, just as the game of sailboat racing requires these same attributes. If you don't try new techniques and develop new skills your level of efficiency will not improve. The more techniques you try and the more techniques you master, the better your chances of winning races and enjoying the sport.

Learn as much as you can from as many people as you can. If possible, ask the winners and leaders of your class why they are making certain adjustments, why they are going to certain areas of the course, and what they find is the best starting technique. Try them yourself and if they work, use them; if they don't work, discard them. As stated, everyone sails his boat differently. What works for someone else may not work for you. Find the techniques, skills and tools which work best for you.

Sailboat racers are a unique breed. The winners and leaders are always trying to help those who wish to learn new skills and techniques. It seems as though they are trying to show other people how it is possible for them to be beaten.

I mentioned the use of a grease pencil to mark down compass bearings, windshifts and other notes on your deck. A grease pencil is very handy. You can write everything from who you are protesting to the slick crew one of your friends is using this weekend. Most important, you can make notes immediately following the race. What items did you overlook for that particular race or that particular race day? Were you constantly sailing high on the reaches, thereby losing several boats, or were you starting at the wrong end of the line?

By constantly reviewing your notes you will soon whittle down your major problem areas and start refining your own style and techniques of winning sailboat races. You will know you are successful when there aren't any boats in front of you at the finish.

Glossary

Apparent Wind: The wind which is propelling the boat. It is the combination of the real wind and the wind created by the speed of the boat moving forward. The tell-tale usually reflects the apparent wind.

Backing Wind: A counter-clockwise shift of the mean wind.

Beating: The art of sailing a boat into the source of the wind by sailing at an angle to it. The art calls for taking advantage of wind shifts and the boat's own ability to sail close to the wind.

Boat Speed: A sailor's reference to a mystical justification of why one boat is faster than another. However, in the real world, what the initials imply.

Boom: The spar at the foot of the sail.

Boom Vang: A piece of equipment which maintains the boom height, mast bend and sail leech tension when the mainsail is eased for off wind sailing.

Clew: Lower, aft corner of the sail.

Cunningham: Sail adjustment which controls the luff tension and draft placement.

Death Roll: A violent motion from side to side caused by the sail being eased forward of the mast.

Draft: The fullness or belly of the sail.

Favored Tack: The tack on which one can sail at a steeper angle and more direct course to the weather mark.

Feathering: The ability to adjust the sail so the boat sails at as small an angle to the wind as possible.

Gust: An area of high energy air or wind.

Header: A wind shift which forces one to leeward, away from the objective.

Hiking: A method of using one's weight as a stabilizing force to prevent excessive heeling.

Hull Trim: Fore and aft and side to side adjustment of the hull in the water.

Jib: Forward sail of a sloop rigged boat.

Jibe: Maneuvering in such a way that the stern of the boat passes through the eye of the wind, and as a result the sail passes across the stern of the boat, often violently.

Lateral Resistance Plane: The emersed area of the board (keel), rudder and hull which prevents the boat from sliding to leeward (sideways).

Leech: The aft edge of the sail.

Lee Helm: The tendency of the boat to sail away from the wind.

Leeward: The direction which is away from the wind.

Leeway: The motion the boat makes as it slides to leeward (sideways).

Lift: A wind shift which allows one to sail closer to the objective, on a more favorable course to the mark.

Luff: Forward edge of the sail.

Luffing: Bringing the boat so high into the wind that the sail loses all its air and power to drive the boat, resulting in a flapping sail.

Mainsheet: The line from the boom which controls sail trim and mast bend.

Mean Wind: The average direction of the wind.

Olympic Course: Type of race course used in Olympic racing: it consists of a triangular course with three beats, two reaches and a run (see Figure 31).

One Minute Rule: IYRU Rule 51.1C. This rule states that all starters must be on the pre-start side of the starting line one minute prior to the start of the race. This rule may be extended to five minutes by the race committee.

Oscillation: Wind shifts rotating on either side of the mean wind.

Outhaul: Sail adjustment at the clew controlling the tension of the foot of the sail along the boom.

Oversheeting: Pulling the sheet and/or traveler in to a point at which the sail ceases to propel the boat.

Phase: The duration of the shifting wind (oscillation) from one direction to its return to that direction.

Reaching: Point of sailing where one is traveling across the wind.

Rhumb Line: Straight line course from one bouy to another.

Roll Tack: An efficient method of coming about from one tack to the other (see Chapter 5).

Round House Lift: A continuous shift caused by a passing weather disturbance.

Rounding Veer: A continuous clockwise shift caused by a passing weather disturbance.

Rounding Back: The same as a rounding veer, only in a counter-clockwise direction.

Running: Point of sailing where one is traveling with the wind, in the same direction as the wind.

Shimming: A method of raising the centerboard whereby one steers slightly into the wind and then off the wind to ease pressure on the board.

Shroud: Wire supports for the mast.

Surfing: A method of using the waves to propel the boat, taking advantage of the speed and kinetic energy of the waves.

Tack: Forward, lower corner of the sail..

Tacking: Changing course so the bow passes through the eye of the wind.

Traveler: A piece of equipment on which the mainsheet rides. It may be located midboom or endboom, depending on the boat. It controls the position of the mainsheet side to side.

Veering Wind: A clockwise shifting wind.

Weather: The windward side of the boat, the direction which is into the wind (as opposed to leeward).

Weather Helm: The tendency of the boat to steer itself into the wind.

Winner: The person who makes the fewest mistakes and has no one finishing in front of him.

Haessner Publishing, Inc.-Information:

This book is part of a continuing project. Please advise us of any additions or corrections which you come across in reading this volume. Any information, no matter how obscure or seemingly unimportant, is welcomed. In sending information, please make reference to the title and author and mail to: **Boating Editor, Haessner Publishing, Inc., Drawer B, Newfoundland, N.J. 07435**